the
sacred
bedroom

ALSO BY JON ROBERTSON

The Sacred Kitchen with Robin Robertson

the
sacred
bedroom

Creating Your Sanctuary for
Spirituality, Sensuality, and Solace

JON ROBERTSON

NEW WORLD LIBRARY
NOVATO, CALIFORNIA

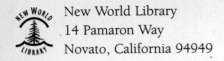

New World Library
14 Pamaron Way
Novato, California 94949

Edited by Georgia A. Hughes and Katharine Farnam Conolly
Front cover design by Mary Ann Casler
Text design and typography by Tona Pearce Myers

The material in this book is intended for education. It is not meant to take the place of evaluation and treatment by a qualified practitioner or therapist. No expressed or implied guarantee as to the effects of the use of the recommendations can be given nor liability taken.

Permissions acknowledgments on page 181 are an extension of the copyright page.

Library of Congress Cataloging-in-Publication Data
Robertson, Jon.
  The sacred bedroom : creating your personal sanctuary / by Jon Robertson.
      p.   cm.
  Includes bibliographical references and index.
  ISBN 1-57731-143-4 (alk. paper)
  1. Bedrooms—Religious aspects. 2. Spiritual life. I. Title.
BL588 .R63 2001
643'.53—dc21   00-013264

First Printing, April 2001
ISBN 1-57731-143-4
Printed in Canada on acid-free paper
Distributed to the trade by Publishers Group West

10 9 8 7 6 5 4 3 2 1

For Robin

CONTENTS

Acknowledgments

For their immeasurable help, I am indebted to my wife Robin Robertson, my editors Georgia Hughes and Katie Farnam Conolly, and my agent Natasha Kern and her staff. Thanks are also due to my friends Tom Ehrhardt for his advice, Carol Haenni for her views on romance, and Samantha Ragan for her assistance with graphics and illustrations.

Introduction

The opportunity to write a book on seeking the sacred in the bedroom has enabled me to share a number of personal discoveries: that many of our most important life-altering experiences occur in the bedroom and that we often encounter Spirit there.

The bedroom may seem a most unexpected place to seek the sacred, but we have overlooked the value of the bedroom as a venue for our connection to the Divine. We spend eight to ten hours there every day, whether in solitude, in prayer, borne aloft in dreams, or making love, and these activities stir the deepest levels of our souls. They light lanterns in our higher consciousness, that part of us that is never out of touch with the Creator.

In this demanding, distracting age, we need to feel that we have access to sacred experiences in every aspect of life, not merely on those occasions when we visit a church, temple, or synagogue. Without sacred experiences, we are swallowed up by our materialistic, demanding world. When we feel no connection to the sacred, we are prone to depression, emptiness, and feeling lost in life. But the bedroom may be our greatest ally in recovering that connection. It is the personal home space to which we return at the end of each day. In the bedroom, we are our most authentic self, being more genuinely who we are and expressing ourselves more honestly than we would ever dare at work, in a place of public worship, or even at the breakfast table with other family members.

In terms of format and style, this book is modeled after *The Sacred Kitchen,*

What we think of as "sacred" actually is present in everything we do.

∞ Riane Eisler

which was coauthored by my wife, author and chef Robin Robertson. In that book, we showed how people can recover the portion of the day spent cooking and eating and use it as a tool for maintaining a spiritual life at mealtime. We showed that food is provided by the Father-Mother Creator, and how to view cooking as a miracle by which life is sustained. We explored how to use meditation and prayer, ceremony, and world traditions to turn cooking into a nurturing, sacred experience. But we all spend far more time in the bedroom than in the kitchen — a third of our lives or more.

Many of my own beliefs converge in this book. What is sacred to me? My life is filled with moments in which I see, touch, taste, smell, or hear the sacred. My heart sings in closeness to God while beholding a sunset from a mountaintop; viewing an artistic masterwork; or listening to a Beethoven symphony. All of these, to me, were inspired by the Creator. People experience the sacred in all sorts of contexts outside of formal religious structures — and they should feel good about doing so. The holy books of ethics-based religions — nearly all of them — are sacred to me, as is prayer, inspired music, and religious customs. They are sacred to me because they are sacred to someone else. This openness enhances my spiritual beliefs and practice.

I believe in the value of meditation — taking time apart from the world and the circus of our own thoughts in order to regularly visit a healing space of peace that resides within us. I believe in the power of prayer for reaffirming our beliefs, petitioning the Highest Power for guidance, and sending energy to people and situations that need help. I also believe in the value of solitude for quieting the nerves and remembering who we are and what we desire to be, even if we are often forced to play other roles. I am also certain, from personal experience, that sexuality, when understood and practiced with a sacred approach, mirrors the nature of our Creator. I believe that true love, spiritual love, is the solution for relationships, good sex, mental health, self-esteem, and that the bedroom is the perfect laboratory in which to develop it. This book explains how to incorporate these concepts into your spiritual life in what I call a "sacred bedroom."

Making practical use of spiritual concepts in the bedroom gives us a great opportunity to keep Spirit alive in our minds and hearts every day. By turning the bedroom into a sacred space, we change the bedroom environment from a place of exhaustion to that of an inspiring temple.

To create a sacred bedroom, you can begin by maximizing the flow of energy in the room and using natural materials in the furnishings and fabrics. Let the décor please the senses through the use of natural materials and essential oil fragrances. Establish an altar to assist in meditation and worship according to your beliefs. Turn your bedroom into a sacred bedroom in your home, and it becomes your personal sanctuary for reflection, prayer, spiritual growth, and emotional healing. In your sacred bedroom, sexuality is dignified as a celebration of the Divine and its pleasures enjoyed as our natural gifts.

As I wrote this book, I was inspired by the challenges of keeping it balanced and practical, giving you sensible information and provoking you to "think outside the box" of your day-to-day assumptions. For example, showing how to use the bedroom for prayer and meditation was easy compared to showing how sex intimately connects us to the image of God or how to use our dreams for guidance. The foundation of the book had to be informative but also hands-on, providing you with exercises and meditations that can help you form some nurturing new habits at bedtime. The book had to carefully measure some unavoidable superficiality, while not bogging down in the academic. I wanted your journey to be stimulating by throwing uncommon light on the bedroom's common surroundings and by providing creative new ideas in a way that will raise your awareness and enhance your spiritual growth.

The material also had to be accessible by people of all faiths, so I have endeavored to keep the language nondenominational (and gender friendly, too). To advocate one religious point of view may demote another, and the point of this book is to help anyone find the sacred in his or her life, whatever their religious preference. By the same token, I tried not to fall into the trap of saying that all religions are essentially the same, because there are vast

In bed we laugh,
in bed we cry;
And, born in bed,
in bed we die.
The near approach
a bed may show
Of human bliss
to human woe.

~ Isaac de Benserade

differences in customs and theology. I have sought to present these sacred bedroom ideas on the common ground by which all people aspire to know and act with love, a common ground that is both spacious and comfortable.

The chapters move progressively from the vast array of bedroom experiences that shape our lives to uncovering some of the forces that have pushed our bedroom activities into the realm of guilt and shame. We then discover some inspiring, historical precedents for creating a sacred bedroom and explore the real meaning of love in the scriptures of the world. I show how we exemplify by our very nature the image of the Creator.

Guidelines are given for setting up your bedroom according to the principles of feng shui, the Chinese art of placement; these principles, if applied, not only promote energy flow but also invite auspicious improvement in various departments of your life. Your décor, arrangement of objects in the room, choice of materials, and items to eliminate from the bedroom are discussed in a section on holistic interior design. You will explore ways in which you can create a visual focus for worship and meditation in the form of an altar. You will see how you can bring into play the rest of your senses with aromatherapy for the bedroom, the use of sound, plants, and natural light.

The activities of the bedroom tend to blend into the background of our lives, but this book shows how our bedroom activities can be used to harmonize body, mind, and spirit. Simple prayer and meditation techniques will help you free yourself from stress and expand your experience with the still place inside you. You are also encouraged to discover for yourself the potential of your alone time — your solitude — and how to use it for personal healing. Your nighttime life of sleep and dreams is extremely important to understand in terms of how it helps you commune with the sacred in your waking life. Simple techniques for gaining guidance from your dreams are provided.

Chapters on love and sex bring the romantic aspects of the sacred bedroom into the spotlight. By contrasting romance with "being in love," the higher, spiritual mode of love, which I call true love, is shown to be the key to lasting pleasure and fulfillment in

---

A sacred place is anywhere you can be alone with your thoughts. It doesn't matter if you are in a crowd of people, in church or in a room by yourself.

∽ Susan Olsen

your bedroom relationships, whether romantic or sexual. Simple ceremonies and rituals are suggested, so you can use your sacred bedroom to symbolically demonstrate the ideals of your beliefs and reaffirm the sacredness of your life.

Sacred sexuality is explored from the point of view of several ancient mystical traditions, with exercises that you can do with your partner. Keeping sacred sexuality free from outside artificial influences of the media and social pressures is encouraged, as well as how to discover the Divine in your partner during sex. Exercises are provided for those who are single, by which they can discover masculine and feminine consciousness within themselves and channel their sex energy creatively.

Finally, the book shows you how to expand the sense of sacredness nurtured in the sacred bedroom for application in the rest of your life, in the household, on the job, and in all your social activities.

I hope that *The Sacred Bedroom* will take its place in your home and your heart as a book of practical value, one holding spiritual secrets through which you can discover freedom of thought and action, and a method for creating a personal sanctuary where you live. Sidebars and marginal quotations from a variety of sources have been carefully chosen to complement the ideas being presented along the way.

I think of *The Sacred Bedroom* as a love poem to all who read it and take it to heart. It is meant to heal centuries-old rifts and habit patterns, to give you a way of establishing a personal sanctuary in the home to help anchor your happiness. I suggest that you curl up in bed with *The Sacred Bedroom* after all the cares of your day are done. Read it alone or aloud with your partner. Practice the exercises and meditations. Above all, try to see your bedroom in a new light and no longer be afraid to commune with the sacred there. My fervent hope is that, whether you are single or with a partner, you will discover true love in your sacred bedroom and enjoy the benefits of higher awareness for the rest of your life.

O bed! O bed!
delicious bed!
That heaven upon earth
to the weary head!

∽ **Thomas Hood,**
"Her Dream"

A Room for the Heart

*The bedroom is shaped by the peace of sleep, the flights of
dream, and the charged energies of sexuality. Despite its quiet image,
the bedroom contains unfathomable mysteries and power.*

— Anthony Lawlor, *A Home for the Soul*

Our most life-changing experiences take place in the bedroom. Many of us
are born there. We cry there, make love there, pray there, and some even
die there. The bedroom is home to our prayers and dreams, our solitude and sexuality. In this inner sanctum, where secrets and spirituality merge, we shed the
masks we wear in our public lives and every night become whole again.

BEDTIME STORY

Whatever occurs during a busy day, we ultimately return to the bedroom
after we leave in the morning. This quiet curtained chamber, with its bed,
dressers, and closets, is where we release a breath at day's end, don a special costume, or go completely naked without a care. For many of us, the bedroom is
our stress-free zone of solitude and relaxation.

Your bedroom is your
place of retreat
and it can symbolize
the way you perceive
your inner self.

∽ Denise Linn,
Sacred Space

The bedroom means different things to different people. It is the place to collapse for those craving sleep; the place to make love for those burning with passion. It is where many of us store our clothes and dress up in them, put on a face, and mentally prepare for the day. It's the room where dust collects under the bed, where laundry piles up, where we write in our journals, or where we try out a new look.

Stop and think of the bedroom's awesome power. We share our love in the bedroom and create life itself there with our bodies and our hearts. So intimate, private, and personal is the bedroom. It is the only space in the house where guests hesitate to wander and where family members enter under strict rules.

We often pray there, soar in orgasm there, and sigh our deepest sighs there. It is perhaps the only place where spirituality, grooming, and sexuality nestle side by side. At its best, the bedroom is a place for union with partner, higher self, and with the Creator in whose image we are made.

The bedroom is where we sleep, where each night our dreams take us into higher worlds. We awaken in the night, sweaty from a nightmare or homesick as some perfect dream begins to fade away. We are sometimes startled awake, inspired with ideas, prickly all over with embarrassment, or unexpectedly stimulated and passionate. Vivid realities return to us of a lost childhood love, some forgotten hot-skinned shame, or a replay of grief for someone who passed away long ago.

Some of us learned to pray as children there, elbows on the bed before sleep, blessing everyone we could think of, asking to pass a test we were dreading the following day at school. As adults, we have knelt down by the bed to pray like we never prayed before: to pass life-or-death tests we did not expect. In the bedroom, we have known the sudden flash of perfect clarity.

The bedchamber is where parents keep secrets from their children, at least for a few years, and where children keep secrets from parents their whole lives. Many of us have been sent there without any supper. Some of us were beaten there, concluding that there was no God at all. The bedroom is where, as kids, we were made to think about what we had done and to make sure we did all our homework. It is where we sulked when we got grounded. We suffered terribly in the bedroom when we were sick, while Mom brought tender words, medicine, tea, and toast. In the bedroom, we have felt the warmth of the sacred.

The bedroom is sometimes a screening room for late-night TV or a sparring ring for bitter and sarcastic arguments. It can be a place for negotiation, for defending personal fortresses, for conquests, treachery, and unions unholy as well as holy. The bedroom is often the place for apologies and forgiveness, a place for solitude when we need to be alone.

Our bedroom experiences propel us toward the sacred because they change us forever. Think of the bedrooms far away where we had to take care of ourselves for the first time. I will never forget how my life changed away at camp in a bunk bed and, later in life, in a sleeping bag under the stars. Can you remember a special night in a hotel, motel, the stateroom on a luxury liner, or something that happened in a sleeping car on a train that altered your life?

Many of us had our first sexual experiences in dormitories away at school. In bedrooms we have had our share of disappointments, narrow escapes, big mistakes, and we have also known some once-in-a-lifetime ecstasies that opened our imaginations and hearts in ways that could never be undone.

Whether you live in an efficiency apartment where the bed pulls down from the wall or in a five-bedroom house by a lake, most of us have a bedroom, from the cradle near Mommy's side to the cemetery on the hill, the final resting place for our worn-out bodies. For these reasons, the bedroom can be considered a sacred place. The bedroom hosts our rites of passage, initiations that test our faith in ourselves, our partners, and in the Creator.

There is a link between what we do in this mystical, powerful space and the harmony or disharmony in our lives. If we rediscover the bedroom through its hidden symbolism, we can begin to heal much of our confusion about life, love, and personal identity. Discovering the potential of the sacred in our bedrooms can help us in every other aspect of our lives. This is what *The Sacred Bedroom* is all about: discovering the sacred potentials

> Wherever you live is your temple if you treat it like one.
>
> ✍ Jack Kornfield,
> *A Path with Heart*

We can never know
God until we first know
clearly our own soul.

∽ Julian of Norwich

in the bedroom activities of sleep, solitude, dreaming, meditation, prayer, sexuality. It is about enhancing our lives by utilizing this undiscovered sacred space to our best advantage, and creating a sacred bedroom in which to strengthen our spiritual life and grow toward the Divine.

MAKING OUR BEDS

Our bedroom experiences tend to shape our happiness: This room is the true home of the heart. We create our spiritual, mental, sexual, and emotional baggage there, not only through what we do, but also through our reflection, brooding, planning, and the choices we make when we are all alone. We use the bedroom as a place of escape, but we could use it instead as a place for extraordinary healing, clarity, recharging, and illumination of our problems and their solutions.

You can evaluate your happiness through the lens of your bedroom life. Do this some evening when you are free from the expectations of others and you can be yourself, in what I call your "bedroom persona." In a relaxed state, begin measuring your happiness by asking yourself some important questions. It will be helpful to write down your answers, perhaps in a journal, so you can review them as you progress in your understanding of the sacred bedroom.

- Am I spiritually healthy?

  Assess whether you feel a direct connection to the Creator and whether your thoughts and actions are conducive or detrimental to your growth. Do you sense that some part of you, a soul perhaps, lives beyond your death? Do you feel that your life serves a greater purpose?

- Am I confident and secure?

  When you go to sleep at night or awaken in the morning, do you feel confident about who you are and secure in your connection to the Divine?

- Do I ever truly relax, even when in solitude?

Are you comfortable spending time alone with yourself, without something to occupy your hands or your mind? Do you enjoy experiencing silence?

- Do I hide my bedroom persona, like the room itself, out of sight?

The person you are when alone in your bedroom can be the same person who goes off to work. Practicing your spirituality in the bedroom can help integrate your whole life in Spirit.

- How does it feel to be in my bedroom?

Do the décor, colors, light, and arrangement give you a relaxing, nurturing feeling? One that helps you feel close to the spiritual principles you live by?

- Is my bedroom merely a closet for my fears, embarrassments, shame, guilt, and secrets?

When some people are alone, their fears rise to the surface, blotting out peaceful thoughts. In your bedroom, you are entitled to feel comfortable and free from negative feelings.

- Do I associate sexuality with happiness?

Whether you are alone or living with a partner, consider that you can attain a more spiritual awareness toward sexuality, and that you can use your bedroom to attain it.

- Am I afraid to associate sex with Spirit?

In the chapters that follow, you will gradually bring the sacred bedroom to life in your home. Along the way, sexuality will be explored as a distinct part of your divine nature.

Your answers to the questions above may reveal some surprising information about your spiritual health, attitudes, and feelings. They reflect some of the most crucial issues in your life, and they are all tied to the bedroom.

If you are like most people, your answers indicate that there is room for improvement. Perhaps a more regular spiritual practice could improve your self-esteem and confidence. If you learned

> The bed, my friend, is our whole life. It is there that we are born, it is there that we love, it is there that we die.
>
> ∽ Guy de Maupassant

how to truly relax, perhaps you could free yourself from the effects of stress. If you understood the sacred connection to sexuality, perhaps you would be more comfortable about it and even more knowledgeable as a lover. Your answers may also indicate something shared by millions of people: a sense of confusion and frustration in the intimacy department — intimacy with others in social and sexual situations but also intimacy with yourself in solitude. For most people, feeling intimacy with the Divine is unexplored territory.

Confusion about intimacy is bound up in our training and its resultant attitudes. As individuals, we really do not know the full extent of who we are. Moreover, our confusion is perpetuated every morning when we dress for the day, because we effectively leave our bedroom persona behind when we go out into the world.

The reasons for this may be unavoidable. Our world is increasingly more hectic and uncertain. Responsibilities and demands on our time have become crushing. We work twice as hard as our parents did to maintain the same quality of life. Even though we enjoy the most prosperous society in the world, there is precious little time for genuine rest, let alone for turning our thoughts to the sacred once we collapse in the bedroom at day's end.

Each morning, we perform a series of rituals in a prescribed order: teeth, shower, hair, choosing a color-coordinated outfit, makeup for women, tying a tie for men, selecting the shoes, and straightening our lines in the mirror. We set ourselves mentally for the day, fixing expressions "just so" for the people we will contact. We do the same for an evening out with friends or to go on a date. Whatever we experienced in the bedroom the night before — dreams, lovemaking, cuddling, or even just a little reading — is forgotten by the time we leave in the morning. We leave the house sporting a personality that we have learned to wear in order to succeed in the world.

We leave the bedroom far behind when we venture out into traffic. We abandon that quiet space that holds our sacred mementos and hears our private thoughts and furtive prayers. However contrite we were last night, sincere, prayerful, or passionate, we

---

Why do some people want to keep the Spirit (God) in the parlor while making love in the bedroom? The best sources seem to suggest that God likes bedrooms, too. In fact — can we possibly emphasize it enough? — God invented the bedroom's activity. So making love can celebrate God's creativity in our own design as human lovers.

∽ Dody H. Donnelly,
Radical Love

cut the emotion off from our consciousness when we step into our roles of the day. Complicating the problem is that we do not play just one role, but many. In effect, we practice, over time, not to be ourselves.

For example, we play a role at our jobs and different roles as mothers, fathers, pals, companions, athletes, corporate officers, secretaries, teachers, even shoppers and commuters. Whatever association we make to the sacred during prayer, meditation, dreaming, and even lovemaking is disconnected by the daytime person who goes off to work to fight the good fight, all to the repression of the complete person that longs for freedom beyond the bedroom door. But this does not have to be so. We can unify ourselves into a healed, happy whole and be that singular person all night and all day, too.

By playing these different roles and putting on all these faces, we eventually begin to believe in them, and this is how we lose touch with our partners and ourselves. We find ourselves feeling cut off from what is meaningful because we do not know how to integrate our bedroom personas with our identities in the outside world.

Our difficulty in reconciling these two apparently opposing identities places genuine intimacy out of reach. Some people spend so little time in the role of the authentic self, they lose touch with who they really are. By honoring the sacredness of the bedroom and forgiving and sanctifying the activities we perform there, we can better know our true selves and recognize our more practical roles for what they are.

Although we play all these roles during the day, once back in the private chamber of the bedroom, we become temporarily whole again. There, we let our emotions break forth upon our faces just as our thoughts inspire them. We grimace in the mirror and make faces that we wouldn't show our families or coworkers. We just do not realize that in this place and time, before leaving from and after returning to the bedroom, we can heal these personas back into one: to be the best, most authentic selves we can be.

We don't realize this because a number of obstacles stand in our way. For starters, we have our fears, doubts, pressures, and the

> For God speaks in one way, and in two, though man does not perceive it. In a dream, in a vision of the night, when deep sleep falls upon men, while they slumber on their beds, then he opens the ears of men.
>
> ✎ Job 33:14–16

In death the many
become one; in life the
one becomes many.

∽ Tagore

worst affliction of all: stress. We have tension, perhaps with a partner, and loads of guilt. Consider, too, how the bedroom has been fitted with so many rules. Think of the contradictions: In the bedroom, a Bible sometimes resides alongside a sexy black negligee. It is the only room in the house where we talk to God while naked or making love!

Spending an hour a week in a place of worship helps the faithful, and an hour a week in a therapist's office helps those whose faith has failed them. Creating a sacred bedroom — one in which your activities are purposeful and cultivated for the purpose of healing and wholeness — can give you the benefit of both, every day and night.

If you have never thought of that, you will enjoy exploring how to use the bedroom to heal your life. You may even discover how to unite your faith, sex, religious practice, solitude, and intimate life — all in the temple of the bedroom. I did it in my life, and it feels wonderful. To begin, you will need a new perspective.

UNDER THE COVERS

Our modern attitude toward the bedroom was shaped by many forces over thousands of years. The bedroom has been a haven for surviving the winter, a setting for politics, and it has been reviled for its proximity to sin. It would seem far removed from the sacred, but we can appreciate the sacred potential of this space when we reflect on its hidden powers.

We make plans in the bedroom and secretly conspire there. We communicate intimately with a partner, for example, hatching some plan for work the following day, anticipating a house move, or making a job change. We win our share of victories in the bedroom, but most of us have never literally conquered an empire there.

Whenever you strategize in the bedroom — whether for turf at work or to win the admiration of a new partner — you are making use of one of its fundamental powers: the power of privacy, in which we let down our guards, establish trust, and induce partners to acquiesce. Peeking under the covers of history, we see how this power has helped steer human destiny.

Breakfast in Bed

Arrange a simple breakfast on a tray, such as tea or cocoa, fresh-squeezed juice, muffins, crumpets, or scones with jam. Or get as elaborate as you like with homemade waffles or pancakes. Whatever you prepare, use the best china and silver, a cloth napkin, and don't forget the newspaper and a fresh flower in a bud vase.

Ambitious Cleopatra decided to revive her fading dynasty in the bedroom by romancing powerful Roman commanders, clients, and allies, including Julius Caesar. Three years after Caesar's assassination, she set her sights on Marc Antony, with whom she whiled away her evenings in rowdy and decadent banquets that kept the citizens of Alexandria awake all night. In August of 30 B.C.E. they committed suicide together — he by falling on his sword and she in bed by the bite of an asp. The Romans and Egyptians alike peopled their bedrooms with images of their many gods of sexuality, fertility, and dreams.

Patrician Romans would not have dreamed of sharing a bedroom with a spouse. Such familiarity would have interfered with a good wife's lovers, let alone the good husband's mobility as a man about town. Her job was to look pretty and not seem too smart, while his was to don toga and sandals and show up at the baths by noon. But that does not mean that the Roman bedroom, in principle, was any less the setting for history-altering events.

This was true out in the Roman provinces. In Judea, for example, Herodias wielded sufficient influence on Herod to persuade him to decapitate John the Baptist after Salome danced her famous dance. The morning Jesus of Nazareth was to be put to death, Pontius Pilate's wife had a dream that augured unspecified mishaps: Perhaps dung fell into the well, a slave spilled unguent into her eyeliner, or a crow flew east to west at the wrong time of day. Whatever the omens, she warned her husband sternly about the significance of the dream, telling him not to have anything to do with Jesus, an innocent man. Thinking he was heeding his wife, Pilate washed his hands of him. His misunderstanding of her bedroom event changed history forever.

In answer to the question, "Why did you create the world?" the Lord said: "You want to know your Lord's meaning in what I have done? Know it well, love was his meaning. Who reveals it to you? Love. What did he reveal to you? Love. Why does he reveal it to you? For love."

∾ Julian of Norwich

The world has order and power and richness that can teach you how to conduct your life artfully, with kindness to others and care for yourself.

~ Chogyam Trungpa
Rinpoche

In medieval times, the bedrooms of Asia hosted ancient spiritual practices. Emperors in China practiced Taoist philosophy, in which their bedroom arts were as crucial to the kingdom's welfare as wars and taxes. Japan's Shinto tradition regarded sexuality as a key element to family happiness and national security. In medieval India, fulfilling *kama*, the desire and need for love, in a room set aside for lovemaking, set the tone for marriages across the land. Harem politics in the Middle East manipulated many a pasha to pass laws, to free or take prisoners, or look the other way at just the right time. The European practice in which the lord of the manor had first dibs on every new bride in the fiefdom, *jus prima noctis,* led to more than one revolution.

History reveals a pattern of polite and impolite arrangements of marriage by which the sovereigns of two nations joined in bed in order to increase their treasuries and merge their armies against mutual enemies. In other situations, a king's lusts drove politics and changed the laws of the land. The case of Henry VIII is a prime example. In order to wed Anne Boleyn in 1533, he broke with the Roman Catholic Church and brought about the English Reformation. Later on, Harry would legalize marriage to first cousins, just so he could marry Catherine Howard.

Anne Boleyn's daughter Elizabeth I began her forty-five-year rule of England in 1558. She was adored by the English during her lifetime and beyond — precisely because she chose to have *no one* share her bedroom. Through her chosen identity as the "Virgin Queen," Elizabeth kept the obedient respect of England throughout her reign. Good Queen Bess was known to have worked often in her four-posted, tented bed and even received ambassadors there.

Another aspect of the bedroom's power is how it inspires creativity. Mozart's *Marriage of Figaro* opens in the bedroom with Figaro taking measurements for his marriage bed. The flamboyant Italian composer Gioacchino Rossini would sometimes sulk bored in bed for days at a stretch. He was so lazy, he would not get up to retrieve a duet that had been blown to the floor by a breeze. He simply wrote it again from memory. Many artists sketched and painted in their bedrooms. Henri Matisse, for example, would lie in bed and draw on his bedside walls using charcoal attached to

Strange Bedfellows

- Alexander the Great occasionally used his bed as a throne.
- Pythagoras had his bed neatened as soon as he arose — for if the impression left by a sleeper's body were stabbed, it was believed, harm could befall him.
- The ninth-century Viking queen Asa was buried with her wooden slatted bed and down coverlets in a boat to carry her to Valhalla.
- Henry VII sprinkled his bed with holy water before retiring, which, unknown to him, only aggravated his rheumatism.
- Charles Dickens could only sleep in a bed aligned on a north-south axis.
- Cardinal Richelieu traveled about solely by bed, demanding that doorways, house walls, and even city gates be demolished to permit his passage.
- Louis XIV once ordered 413 beds, including the great bed at Versailles, inscribed in gold: "The Triumph of Venus." He even dispensed justice from this bed.
- Napoleon insisted on sleeping in total darkness, which Josephine could not stand.
- Milton, Voltaire, Mark Twain, George Sand, and Elizabeth Browning all wrote in bed.
- Casanova would set a clock charged with gunpowder to wake him promptly from strange beds.
- Benjamin Franklin slept in two beds each night. He would switch to the second after the first became too warm.
- In a bedroom in Belgium, the dancer/counterspy Mata Hari passed military secrets between the French and Germans during World War I.
- The assassination of Archduke Franz Ferdinand, which started World War I, was foretold in a dream received by Bishop Joseph Lanyi.

President Lyndon B. Johnson used dreams throughout his career.

the end of a long cane. A famous photograph pictures Samuel Clemens in bed, where he wrote a number of his books.

The bedroom is humankind's workshop and proving ground for relationships. As such, it is a key player in our mental and emotional health. Our misunderstanding of the power of the bedroom may have direct bearing on why 43 percent of American women and 31 percent of men experience sexual dysfunction and why we consume most of the world's psychotropic drugs just to get through the day. By itself, even a sacred bedroom cannot reverse an underlying spiritual poverty created by ancient suppressive attitudes mixing with the unrealistic expectations of romance and lovemaking depicted in the media. Our bedroom activities are affected by these influences, whether we realize it or not.

Our attitude toward the bedroom, and what we do there, was premeasured for us centuries ago by religious doctrines. It is not that we revile the bedroom or its potential to be a healing force in our lives; we unconsciously associate it with sin and guilt.

The fourth century gave us Augustine, whose writings inspired a host of rules and guidelines that pushed the bedroom, and by association its activities, into the doghouse of the subconscious mind.

Prominent religious commentator and former Roman Catholic nun Karen Armstrong wrote on this in *A History of God.* "Augustine believed that God had condemned humanity to an eternal damnation, simply because of Adam's one sin. The inherited guilt was passed on to all his descendants through the sexual act, which was polluted by what Augustine called 'concupiscence.' Concupiscence was the irrational desire to take pleasure in mere creatures instead of God; it was felt most acutely during the sexual act, when our rationality is entirely swamped by passion and emotion, when God is utterly forgotten and creatures revel shamelessly in one another."

The bedroom was mute victim to complicated sets of laws and dogmas established by government and church. Apparently, by this time, the bedroom's potential and power to corrupt had come under scrutiny since Cleopatra's day, revealing a need for laws to govern morality.

The earliest known laws governing sex date from the second millennium B.C.E. in the Near East and pertain to acts or the circumstances under which certain acts are performed. Some of the earliest sex laws appear in Leviticus, Numbers, and Deuteronomy.

Bedtime Story

In some early communal houses the men's bed was separated from the women's bed by a door. Later beds made use of ropes or thongs to hold the sleeper off the ground. Some used forked branches and a frame of thin tree trunks on which to string thongs and stack a "mattress" of skins.

These laws influenced later church laws. Where the old Jewish laws went so far as to say a young man who marries should take a year off work to enjoy his wife and create children, the Christian church encroached deeply into our natural right to enjoy the pleasures of sex.

Sex laws are necessary to keep society orderly, bloodlines pure, and to protect those who cannot protect themselves, such as women and children. Other laws forbid obscene public displays, annoying solicitations, and the spread of disease. However, much of the resulting dogma was not for the protection of person or property, but for enforcing Augustinian morality.

The Victorians observed a catechism of rules and rigors dictating proper sexuality, but unfortunately created a subculture for unspeakable behavior. The suppression, particularly of women in Victorian times, created a repressed womanhood that gave rise to the suffrage movement along with proliferation of brothels. Despite the Women's Movement, women (and men, too) are still working toward freeing themselves from the extremes of generations ago.

All over Europe and North America, Victorian men traveled about visiting bordellos, where, for a few pence, a glass of absinthe and a virgin could be had. This was also the time of Jack the Ripper. French author Gustave Flaubert summed up the results of Victorian morality on the men of his time saying, "A man has missed something if he has never woken up in an anonymous bed beside a face he'll never see again, and if he has never left a brothel at dawn feeling like jumping off a bridge into the river out of sheer physical disgust with life."

At all costs, Victorians protected appearances, because if some indiscretion were found out, the resulting gossip could reflect poorly on a wife, ruin a marriage, create scandal in the community, or condemn individuals to reputations of hysteria, wantonness, or madness. The suppressive Victorian mores created misery for wives, who were expected to behave with the highest moral conduct in and out of bed, while it created an underground of self-indulgence that obeyed no rules. Our modern attitudes toward the bedroom still bear the marks of Victorian hypocrisy.

For all our openness and supposed sexual revolution, the

René Descartes pursued mathematics and philosophy because of his dreams, which led him to propose that through mathematics all the sciences could unite.

∽

Eskimos once carved a ledge of ice and then covered it with furs to create a large communal bed.

United States has far more extensive laws governing sex and morality than many other parts of the world. Unlike modern Europe, U.S. society has held on to many outdated puritanical attitudes. Suppression of sexuality under the guise of morality tends to spawn secret societies, or, at best, trap desires in the subconscious. A code of morality protects society from descending into the depths of unbridled debauchery, but feelings of shame in the bedroom preempt us from enjoying its sacred powers.

One might assume that our modern world is safely in the hands of genteel, gray-suited businesspersons who use science and statistics to call the shots. After all, unlike the days of Marc Antony and Cleopatra, when leaders were praised for the debaucheries of their all-night parties, we are now sophisticated and refined, perhaps even a little bored with an apparently sensible world that settles each night into a queen-sized Perfect Sleeper with two nightstands, twin reading lamps, and matching drapes and spread.

Whether it is our Porsche-driving patrician couples or our plebeian brides and grooms who people the fast-food restaurants and factories of the nation, we still use our bedrooms for politics and building empires.

In 1987 philandering candidate Gary Hart was drummed out of the presidential race for a boat ride to Bimini with a woman who was not his wife; in 1995 Oregon senator Robert Packwood was forced to resign for sexually harassing subordinates; in 1999 Robert Livingston had to step down as speaker of the house before he had even begun — over an old affair revealed by self-proclaimed "investigative pornographer" Larry Flynt. President Bill Clinton was impeached that same year after apparently bedroom testing the Oval Office with an intern. He wasn't the only president to allow supporters to sleep in Lincoln's bedroom in the White House for a night.

Whether your bedroom is a political playing field, a temple of love, or just a place where laundry piles up, our modern world, expectations, conditioning, as well as the mistakes we make there, affect the empires of our lives. We alter there forever the personal histories we write for ourselves, line by line. With all this potential for power, what would happen if we added to the bedroom the element of the sacred? Instead of winning or losing the kingdoms of our desires, perhaps we would find ways to heal our lives, and integrate our sexuality and spiritual lives in ways we have never done before.

Every one of us learns the rules as we are growing up, as much by what we are taught as by what we observe (and do not observe) in our families and in the world around us. But our neglect of the bedroom as a place of honor in the household is not due to the morality laws, even though they have contributed to many psychological and spiritual conflicts. Our neglect of the bedroom is due to an attitude that teaches us to just "get through the night" in the same way that we "get through the day." It is also due to limitations in our understanding of our innate connection to the Divine — God within Us.

The roadblocks are many, but most psychological and religious authorities recommend an active spiritual life in which we can recover the sacred in every natural aspect of our lives. The omission of the sacred from the bedroom is one of the most obvious obstructions to our feeling unity with the Divine. The sacred bedroom can be a powerful solution for recovering a spirituality that is complete, embracing the multiple dimensions of our being. Let us draw the covers down and awaken to a whole new venue for spiritual growth.

> Ancient wisdom shouldn't be ignored simply because it's ancient....
>
> ✎ Robert L. Van de Castle,
> *Our Dreaming Mind*

RISE AND SHINE

The time has never been better for strengthening our belief systems, whatever our particular house of worship. With all the distractions and pressures we face, drawing on the Divine may be more of a necessity than ever before.

During the last third of the twentieth century, an explosion of interest in ancient philosophical ideas raised Westerners' curiosity about life's deeper mysteries. They prodded people to question attitudes toward gender roles, moral dogmas, sexual practices, and religious beliefs. This introspection has had mixed results, but, as individuals, we have never been better equipped to strengthen our

In returning and rest
you shall be saved.
In quietness and in trust
shall be your strength.

∽ Isaiah 30:15

faith, cut through the red tape, and create a more genuine relationship with the Creator.

Many people pray more actively at home than previous generations, not relying solely on formal services as they once did. Others have learned to discipline their minds through meditation and simplify their lives, improve their diets, and try to separate the genuine from the artificial. Some have created sanctuaries within their homes where they pray or meditate. With so many demands on our time, creating a home sanctuary may not only be practical, but could become vital in the coming years.

A home sanctuary would ideally be a space reserved for private matters of spirit: prayer and meditation. It would have comfortable chairs, perhaps a rug, maybe even an altar. It would be a space protected from other activities, where all things holy, the sacred aspects of our lives, could be played out without interference from other family activities. The bedroom, our most private space, is ideal as a home sanctuary. It is the room in which we are our most authentic selves; where we can speak our heart's desires; where we can bring into the light our most intimate experiences.

Whether a partner slumbers beside you or you sleep alone, you can feel truly safe in the bedroom, drifting off to sleep with a prayer on your lips, reviewing the performances of the day, dropping your disguises and perhaps some of the pretenses. There, after the lights go out, you resume that intimate dialogue with your best self, chastise your dark side, and try to reassure the Creator that you are still in there trying.

As we have seen, the secular power of the bedroom in our lives and world history is clear. Its influence is borne out in a litany of liaisons, between husbands and wives, lovers, politicians, kings, and queens. But over the centuries, we have acquired a cabinet of spiritual resources from religious, philosophical, and psychological sources that used to be the sole domain of clerics and sages. With these resources, we can bring beauty and healing into every aspect of our lives. These resources, perhaps surprisingly, belong in the bedroom, and always have:

• *Solitude:* In which we shut out the noisy world that competes for our attention

- *Prayer:* In which we talk to God in private

- *Meditation:* That interior space in which we listen for the answers to our prayers

- *Intimacy:* Whether making love, having a conversation, or being by oneself

- *Lovemaking:* In which we share in the creative forces that brought us into being

- *Sleep:* Where we spend a third of our lives living in the world of our dreams

- *Retreat:* In which we enjoy reflection, recharging, and self-therapy

We will look at each of these functions in the light of one incontrovertible fact: We draw close to the Divine in the bedroom because we talk to God more freely there than in any other place — even a house of worship. In the bedroom, we are alone with our most private thoughts. We face our morality there as well as our mortality:

- "Oh God!" becomes a sigh of relief whispered at the end of a good day.

- Our heads softly cradled in a pillow, we pray, "Oh God!" giving thanks for a child returned home safely.

- We pray: "Oh God! Please . . ." provide a special favor, promotion, or phone call.

- We sing "Oh God!" ascending in a sexual crescendo; cry "Oh God!" during climax, when no other words upon the lips will do.

We can take advantage of our many intimacies by enhancing the environment of the bedroom, gracing it with the symbols of our faith, and allowing the conjugal bed to glow proudly as a site of our most blissful act of creation. Every reader can let that black negligee justifiably coexist with the family Bible, and, yes, with the lights on. We can let this most intimate chamber live in the light and receive us as honored priests or priestesses, rather than as haggard refugee from the ravages of the day. We can let the bedroom proudly take a more exalted place in the house. We can also discover how to let its

We are such stuff
As dreams are made of,
and our little life
Is rounded with a sleep.

    ⤷ Shakespeare,
The Tempest

functions expand to reflect the importance and diversity of all that takes place there. We can create a colorful dais for lovemaking; an altar for worship; a bright sunny corner for meditation, prayer, and reflection. We can make of the bedroom a room for the heart, and all that takes place there in our life can take on a vibrant new meaning.

When lovemaking is planned as part of worship and study, we will learn to feel the holiness of bliss. In this busy world seemingly lost in fear, neuroses, and mixed messages, we truly can turn the bedroom into a templelike haven dedicated to healing and prayer in which lovemaking is blessed in the sight of God. The answers are clearly stated in the sacred literature of the world: love letters, at our fingertips, of all that God has said to humankind since the beginning.

Whether you're a king or queen, a prince or princess, a pawn or a pawnbroker, it's a safe bet that sanctifying this space, airing it out, letting the sunshine in, and making it an honored temple in the house can add many pluses to our spiritual ledgers after all is said and done. The way is easier once we realize that our affairs of the heart are closer to our affairs of spirit than we realize.

IN SEARCH OF THE SACRED

Whenever I visit a large city, I try to spend some time in a cathedral. I appreciate the majestic vaults, brilliant windows, the mystical elements of its design, and the sheer labor it took to construct the huge edifice. Standing in the great vaulted nave, I am overwhelmed by the faith of those who sustain it. In my twenties I found that "cathedral feeling" welling up inside me in unusual places. I began to feel close to the Creator whenever I saw a house of worship — whose ever it was — and it troubled me at first. Was it wrong to feel close to the sacred outside of my childhood place of worship?

I underwent an awakening by which I began to understand similarities that unify the world's faithful. I began to study the scriptures of other lands and looked beyond our religious differences. The broader view strengthened my own faith, because it gave me a new perspective on my beliefs and practices. I found the same respect in my heart for church, mosque, stupa, synagogue, *zendo,* and temple.

God is everything that is good, as I see it, and the goodness that everything has is God.

∽ Julian of Norwich

I have enjoyed that exhilarating "cathedral" feeling while listening to an inspired Baptist minister relate a personal experience to a passage in the Bible. I have felt it when a Catholic priest holds high the Holy Eucharist, a tiny bell ringing the presence of Christ for the faithful. I have felt it hearing a cantor sing in Hebrew. I have felt this closeness of Spirit at a Friends meetinghouse, the Quakers standing when moved to speak from the heart. I have also felt it at an ashram, during a silent retreat, or borne aloft amid Sanskrit chants of praise for the effulgent light at the core of all being. I have felt God's touch while being embraced by a Tibetan Buddhist lama and while enjoying dinner prepared by a Japanese Buddhist priest, and serving a kosher meal to a Hasidic rabbi.

We can live a more balanced, satisfying life if we have regular contact with sacred places and things. Modern research has revealed that people who have a religious practice tend to live longer than those who do not. Without a sense that there is a divine force or higher power to give us context within the infinite, there would be little reason to look beyond greed and the base pleasures of life.

Whatever our particular faith, if we are going to find meaning in the sacred bedroom, we need to know what we mean by "sacred." It is important to our sacred bedroom, because we tend to take the sacred for granted. Most of us are taught as children what to hold sacred and few question these teachings: either to revise the assumptions or to bring them more vibrantly to life.

What is sacred to one person is not sacred to another. For example, when the name of God must be written down on paper, an orthodox Jew writes "G-d," for this holy name would be desecrated should the piece of paper be crumbled up and thrown away. A phallic lingam symbol would be repellent to a Christian, but is held as sacred to the Hindu. Mecca is sacred to the Muslim, but just another place on the map to a Buddhist. To many, nature is sacred. I hold the very beating of a heart as a sacred symbol for the Creator's fingerprint: life itself.

Sacred is anything dedicated to the worship of Deity. It is anything set apart for service or worship to God or deemed worthy of veneration. What is sacred is sacred because it is sacred to someone.

> Your old men shall dream dreams, your young men shall see visions.
>
> ✑ Joel 2:28

The revelation here is that whatever you hold sacred, you can bring it to life in a meaningful way in the most intimate room in the house: the bedroom, where we have many sacred experiences throughout our lives.

Sacred objects and places differ among people, but our experiences of the sacred share a common bond. Spirit sweetens our lives with experiences of the Divine, oftentimes when we least expect it. Countless stories exist of angelic intercessions, a profound dream, or a comforting voice during moments of extreme joy, terror, or loss.

Experiences are sacred when they stir the mind with awe and fill the heart with love and gratitude. Ironically, when people sit in a formal house of worship, communing with the sacred can be furthest from their minds. But genuine sacred experiences convey a sense of peace, open a channel of energy from beyond the individual, and bolster our sense of hope. They help us find freshness in every moment and comfort us with the knowledge that some part of us is eternal. Finding even a few moments every day in which to purposely engage in spiritual practice, no matter how informal, helps us live a richer and more meaningful life.

Regardless of how we experience the sacred in our lives, we can acknowledge it, know it, accept it, and be nourished by it wherever we go and whatever we do, simply by looking at life with newly opened eyes to the possibilities. This is true out in the world, but especially in our homes, where we tend to take things for granted. In the bedroom, we can be most open to sacred experience. Our thoughts, feelings, contemplation, and dreams are more intimate there than in a house of worship. Karen Armstrong supports this argument, writing in *A History of God:* "Enlightenment can be nurtured in a monastery or in a family, alone or in a relationship, in prayer or at work."

I have had many experiences in my bedroom that I consider sacred. During meditation or in dreams, I have seen transcendent scenes and symbols, sensed prophets and angels near by, and received messages that proved vital in decisions I was making in my life. These experiences of the sacred helped me in ways that I know were not merely figments of my imagination. But I believe

I do not believe that
I am now dreaming but
I cannot prove I am not.

∾ Bertrand Russell

we all receive such experiences without realizing it. We only become aware of them when we begin looking for sacred experiences in everyday life.

The depth and intensity of our sacred bedroom experiences can be awakened in an awareness of our own sacred nature. The secret is contained in the meaning of the "image of God" in which we are made.

"And God said, Let us make man in our image, after our likeness. . . ." (Genesis 1:26)

The notion that we are patterns of the Divine is echoed throughout the range of human religious literature. Just what is this "image" of God in whose likeness we were created? For the purposes of *The Sacred Bedroom,* the answer comprises three elements:

- The name I AM THAT I AM

- The principle that God-Is-Love

- Our maleness and femaleness

Imagine if you could sit down with the Creator face-to-face for an exact explanation of the "divine image." That is just what Moses did. He received a startling answer from the bush that burned with fire but was not consumed: "I AM THAT I AM," Moses was told. He was told to "say unto the children of Israel 'I AM hath sent me unto you.'" (Exodus 3:14)

This strange answer is either exceedingly simple or deliberately unfathomable. I think it is wiser to choose the simple: I AM is the purest declaration of existence, without regard to conditions, character, intent, purpose, or any other sort of identity. I AM is complete. It is consciousness pure, even without a thought to think. It is awareness of *being* itself without objects or subjects to interfere. I AM is the omniscient statement, definition, and condition of the oneness of awareness shared by all who are aware. The secret to understanding it is knowing merely that all sentient beings are conspicuous disclosures of I AM, whether we realize it or not. Perhaps René Descartes got it backwards. It is not "I think, therefore I am," but "I am, therefore I think."

If consciousness continues after the body dies, then I AM

Be still and know
that I am God.

🙰 Psalm 46:10

never dies, is never wasted, and can never go away. At face value, this self-defined image of God is the very name of consciousness that we all unknowingly pronounce every time we say or even think: I AM. I am ready. I am tired. I am in love. To understand I AM consciousness, think of Huston Smith's words in *Forgotten Truth*: "The brain breathes mind like the lungs breathe air." Consciousness itself is an open circuit to the mind of the Creator.

The second element of the "image of God" is love. Where I AM THAT I AM is simply the state of being aware, love is the active energy radiating from I AM. It is the key to perceiving our true nature. Love is the pattern and foundation of our souls that forever links the Creator with the created.

Teachings on the Creator as love flow from every religion. "God is love," wrote John, "and he that dwells in love dwells in God." (1 John 4:16) The Upanishads make many references to love: "True religion is to love, as God has loved them, all things, whether great or small." (The Hitopadesa) The *Sutta Pitaka* of Buddhism asserts: "The ninth perfection is loving-kindness." The *Tao Te Ching* offers: "World sovereignty can be committed to that man who loves all people as he loves himself." These are the love letters from a Creator that has repeated the message, through all the prophets, from the beginning: God-Is-Love.

Love manifests in how we treat each other. We all perform loving acts — unplanned kindnesses to family members, coworkers, lovers, even to strangers at the supermarket. This basic goodness in people reflects the harmony in nature and the loving heart of the Creator, which manifests everywhere, unless preempted by human folly.

The great secret of love is the freedom and relief you can know in just forgetting about yourself for a little while. In that state you can send and receive (prayer and meditation) to a much greater effect. You can also sleep better and make love better knowing that God-Is-Love is a part of you. In the state of selfless love, in your sacred bedroom sanctuary, you can find the image of God within you and elevate every aspect of your life simply by opening your heart to love. God Is Love. I AM THAT I AM.

You are the content of your consciousness; in knowing yourself, you will know the universe.

∽ J. Krishnamurti

God-Is-Love

Christianity: "Judge not, and you will not be judged; condemn not, and you will not be condemned; forgive, and you will be forgiven; give, and it will be given to you...." (Jesus, Luke 6:27)

Buddhism: "All men shrink from suffering and all love life; remember that you too are like them; make your own self the measure of others, and so abstain from causing hurt to them." (Dhammapada)

Judaism: "What is hateful to you, do not to your fellow man; that is the entire law; all the rest is commentary." (Hillel)

Islam: "Do to all men as you would wish to have done unto you; and reject for others what you would reject for yourselves." (Hadith)

Hinduism: "Do not to others what you do not wish done to yourself; and wish for others too what you desire and long for, for yourself — this is the whole of dharma, heed it well." (Mahabharata)

Confucianism: "Do not unto others what you would not have them do unto you." (Analects)

Whether it is self-love, Divine love, love of partner, family love, or love of humankind, what do these expressions of love have in common? Why should we expect love to unleash the potential of the sacred bedroom and life in general? I believe that your experiences of love will grow if you apply the principles of this book.

The third aspect of the image of God is our maleness and femaleness. This aspect also has a direct bearing on our most private thoughts and actions in the bedroom. As we contemplate an inspiring new use for the bedroom, men and women need to realize that God is not a *he:* God contains the qualities of both masculine and feminine. It says so in the Bible and many other scriptures.

Most people are not aware that in Genesis, "man" is initially created male and female.

And God said, Let *us* make man in *our* image, after *our* likeness.... So God created man in his *own* image, in the

In the beginning there was nothing but Self, in the shape of a person. But Self felt no delight in the void and wished for a second. Self then fell into two, and thence arose husband and wife. "We two are thus, each of us, like half a shell." He embraced her, and humanity was born.

∽ The Upanishads

image of God created he him; *male and female created he them.* (author's italics) Genesis 1:26–27

The use of the plural "us" does not mean that the Creator is two instead of one. It merely reflects that God contains and encompasses our own duality of male and female. The sense of Spirit in our maleness and femaleness is restated in Genesis 5:2:

Male and female created he them; and blessed them, and called their name Adam, in the day when they were created.

We human males and females — by our very gender — are reflected in the image of God. Moreover we each have a masculine and feminine nature within us, regardless of whether we live in a male or female body. Even with these dual qualities, each individual soul, like the Creator, is One. This opens a powerful door to self-discovery available to us in the sacred bedroom, particularly in terms of our sexuality.

There are many creation accounts throughout the world, metaphysical sources, and scriptures in addition to the Bible that support this idea. In Hinduism, the dual-gender nature of God corresponding to the Genesis description of male and female is depicted in the principles of Shiva (male) and Shakti (female). These deities represent balance within the individual, union between the soul and the Creator, as well as sexual union in all its divine characteristics: procreation, love, unity, ecstasy.

Taoist philosophy acknowledges masculine and feminine as yin (feminine) and yang (masculine), perfect harmony expressed through the coexistence of opposites, yet contained in the single yin-yang symbol. (See Figure 1.1.) Taoists believe that in sexual union the divine is achieved as these two great forces join and that the man and woman exchange the complementary energies through their bodies. English Christian mystic Julian of Norwich wrote in her *Revelations of Divine Love* that God is both father and mother. Kabbalah, Judaism's mystical tradition, ascribes masculine and feminine qualities to the two main pillars of the tree of life: *binah* and *hochmah*.

> The bed has become a place of luxury to me! I would not exchange it for all the thrones in the world.
>
> ∽ Napoleon

Yin and Yang literally mean the "dark side" and "sunny side" of a hill. The symbol depicts the dualistic nature of all things, uniting in the one Way, or Tao. It is an emblem that evokes the harmonious interplay of all pairs of opposites in the universe.

Figure 1.1

The meaning of "image of God" comes into focus as awareness of self in the name I AM THAT I AM. That God contains our masculine and feminine qualities, the forces that drive romance and marriage, a tangible picture of God comes to life in the very core of our being.

People are often startled to realize that our maleness and femaleness are reflections of the image of God. By extension, our very sexuality would appear to be divinely ordained. The fact is, the world's scriptures provide a foundation for making the bedroom a temple in which worship and lovemaking can lie down together, side by side. We can do this in a way that does not offend our belief systems, by looking at the traditions that link these bedroom activities to the sacred.

It is ironic, if not humorous, that our spirituality and sexuality live in the same room, but are afraid to look at each other with the lights on. After all, we often pray in the bedroom. We pray for favors and for healing for ourselves and others. We pray for blessings or for disappointments to be taken away. We pray in gratitude and also desperation. We call out the name of God during lovemaking. The prayers of our bedroom may be the most sincere prayers we utter. However, our connection to the sacred in the bedroom goes beyond prayer. We also sleep our sacred sleep, dream our dreams, commune with the Divine in solitude, and make love with our beloved partners.

Little more is as natural or taken for granted in our lives as turning in for the night, but we could heal ourselves and our world if we paid more attention to the potential of this most important of rooms. The next time you retire for the night, enter

True religion is to love, as God has loved them, all things, whether great or small.

    ❧ **The Hitopadesa**

Is it not written in your law, "I said, ye are gods"?

⤳ John 10:34

your bedroom feeling entitled to commune with the Highest Power. Whether you are seated in meditation or tucked into bed for the night, be aware of the I AM consciousness, which is naturally open, receptive, and giving. Be aware that God-Is-Love has been within us from the beginning. Remember that each of us is a masculine-feminine lover full of compassion and one with the Creator.

In the bedroom, you can rest and recharge, talk to Spirit, express love in its many dimensions, and honor your genuine self — your soul — in the knowledge that you (and each person) contain and are made up of the image of God. Set your own rules, based on what you hold sacred in your life, and let the bedroom be your private space in which you rejoice in the divine identity of your authentic self. Let's take a closer look at the bedroom space itself so we can begin to expand our bedroom consciousness and discover a new potential for healing in our life.

Recipes for the Bedroom

Keep a favorite snack in your bedroom for the next time you are sent to bed without any supper:

Private-Stash Trail Mix

In a large bowl, combine equal parts of almonds, walnut pieces, soy "nuts," pumpkin seeds, sunflower seeds, raisins, and carob chips. Mix well and transfer to a plastic sandwich bag, where it will keep for a few days at room temperature.

2

Love's Sacred Spaces

Every person needs a retreat, a "dynamo" of silence,
where he may go for the exclusive purpose of being
newly recharged by the Infinite.

— Paramahansa Yogananda

Begin to create your bedroom sanctuary by harmonizing the physical space itself. Choose natural materials, furnishings, and fabrics, and eliminate toxic chemicals and electromagnetic radiation. Enhance the flow of a hidden energy called *ch'i* through feng shui, the ancient Chinese art of placement, and you have set the stage for a new way to commune with the Divine.

THE HOLISTIC BEDROOM

Whether you conduct your spiritual life in a house of worship or through some personalized practice, if you make your bedroom a sacred space, you can increase your spiritual activity from once or twice a week to fully one-third of your life: the amount of time you spend there.

Even the common articles made for daily use become endowed with beauty when they are loved.

∽ Soetsu Yanagi

Because of its inherent privacy, intimacy, and primal functions, the bedroom provides an ideal venue for bolstering your spiritual life. We can take advantage of it by making the bedroom healthful, harmonizing its furnishings, conditioning its subtle energies, and establishing a spiritual focus. Essentially, we want to create a nighttime environment with the Divine in mind; one that adds a sacred touch to all our bedroom activities: sleep, dreams, prayer, meditation, and sexuality.

The first step is to make sure your bedroom promotes good health. In medicine, a holistic approach looks beyond symptoms to ensure that treatments will support the whole body. A holistic approach to your bedroom, therefore, will have a positive effect on the quality of your life, your connection to the Divine, and your physical and mental health.

In her book *Holistic Home: Creating an Environment for Physical and Spiritual Well-Being,* Joanna Trevelyan recommends a holistic approach to everything we place in the bedroom. Since our physical and emotional health are at stake, it is important to look carefully at the quality of the materials that we bring into the bedroom: what the bed and bedding are made of, the objects that you will hang on the walls or position on the dresser. With deliberate intent, every aspect of the room can be a reminder and celebration of the Divine. At the same time, we want to eliminate sources of physical (and even mental) toxicity from this sacred space. We spend so much time in the bedroom, it should be the least toxic room in the house.

Unfortunately, many of our modern conveniences add toxicity to a room. Formaldehyde wafts from plastic wall coverings, wood paneling, synthetic carpets, and compressed particle and fiberboard. Many synthetic fabrics, found in curtains, draperies, and bed clothing, are treated with chemicals that further poison the space of your bedroom. Such chemicals add mild toxicity to the air, and can be major health risks for people who suffer from environmental illness. As your bedclothes (spreads, sheets, pillow cases, et cetera) are literally "in your face" all night long, consider laundering them with nonallergenic detergents. (See the Resource Directory at the end of the book.)

The process of redecorating your bedroom can be simple and easy, unless your bedroom is in need of major remodeling. The first goal is to replace the toxic materials with natural nonallergenic fibers such as cotton, linen, silk, and wool. Try to use natural woods and eliminate composite materials and plastics, including foam cushions and pillows, polyester, and blends often used in the making of sheets and other bed clothing. This is good advice for the entire house, as chemicals tend to deteriorate our general health.

If your bedroom is carpeted, consider a bare wood floor, because you can never get carpeting completely clean of molds and dust mites. Carpeting, as well as plywood and particleboard, are also known for "outgassing," in which gases from chemical processing escape long after the items have been installed. An excellent solution is to strip and sand the floor and either leave it bare or use a nonplastic varnish, such as shellac, beeswax, or a penetrating finish, such as linseed oil. This keeps the natural look and energy of the wood involved with the space and eliminates the toxicity and outgas tendency of plastic. Place natural fiber area rugs over high-wear areas. Whenever possible during the day, flood the bedroom space with natural light. Adding a skylight above the bed can have a relaxing effect. Try to use full-spectrum incandescent or fluorescent bulbs in your bedroom, as they are known to lift the spirits.

With natural materials in place and toxicity minimized, focus next on enhancing the functions of the bedroom. This involves keeping your bedroom space clear of unnecessary items or items that detract from sacred purposes. Try not to let the bedroom double as an office, workroom, or sewing room. Banish the laundry hamper and ironing board. If you have images or mementos that evoke sadness or loss, consider putting them away for a time, to see if this simple step can change your mood. Give prominence to photos of loved ones and other cherished objects that lift your spirits. Taking these steps will not only help you keep mindful of your bedroom's higher purposes, it can free up precious floor space.

Keep your bedroom private, even among the members of your household. It is your personal sanctuary, so you want to protect it

During the 1940s, Indian mathematician Srinivasa Ramanujan was regularly instructed in his dreams by the Hindu goddess Namakkal, who showed him formulae that he would prove upon waking.

from being the setting for mundane activities, or worse, the scene for an argument or other negativity that you may associate it with later. In the sacred bedroom, be your authentic self, your best self. Your bedroom will become a place of veneration and respect. It is the home of your own sacred identity: I AM THAT I AM.

Another important consideration is to eliminate electromagnetic fields (EMFs) generated by electrical equipment such as TVs, computers, stereos, radios, and hair dryers. EMFs can aggravate stress and stimulate allergies.

Victoria Moran, author of *Shelter for the Spirit: How to Create Your Own Haven in a Hectic World,* writes, "The bedroom should be free from every nonessential electrical accoutrement. For starters, replace your plug-in clock with a battery-operated one. Recharge your cell phone in another room. Metal bed frames, such as brass and other metals, basically act as antennas and induct/conduct EMFs. So skip the brass in favor of good old wood."

EMFs aside, watching TV at bedtime stimulates the brain in ways that can make it difficult to fall asleep and either disturb or influence your dreams. TV messages and imagery can negatively affect your experience of sex, too, because the seductive pictures and sounds unavoidably influence your subconscious mind. It is far better to finish watching TV an hour before bed, using the interim to relax and disengage the mind, perhaps with a cup of tea or some quiet meditation or contemplation. If you enjoy music in your bedroom, be sure to turn off the stereo before you go to sleep, as the sound stimulates portions of the brain that also need rest.

How we decorate the bedroom, and, for that matter, the entire house, is a personal affair, but however you do it, know that you are strongly affected by your surroundings. In her book *House as a Mirror of Self: Exploring the Deeper Meaning of Home,* University of California professor Clare Cooper Marcus writes, "Nesting, homemaking is a major means of personal expression and development. We create our immediate environment and then contemplate it and are worked on by it. We find ourselves mirrored in it, see what had been not yet visible, and integrate the reflection back into our sense of self."

It would be inappropriate for this book to attempt to dictate

Both our Substance and Sensuality together may rightly be called our Soul. That is because they are both oned in God.

෴ Julian of Norwich

decorating specifics, so either trust your instincts and feelings or consult a decorating book or expert. Use your artistic sense on color combinations, window treatments, and bedclothes. Lighten up and harmonize the colors of your walls, spread, and drapes. In *The Western Guide to Feng Shui,* Terah Kathryn Collins recommends making sure soft shapes outnumber sharp corners in furnishings and accessories. For colors, she recommends light yellow to deep gold, light pink to deep red, café au lait to chocolate brown. "Dominating with black, white, gray and many blue tones drops the perceived temperature of the room, when what you really need is warmth for coziness and heat for libido."

Now, let's look at the present configuration of your bedroom, beginning with the bed. Observe the direction your bed faces and its relative position to the door. Try to visualize the bed's ancient, universal symbolism. Your bed is primal. Whether on a rude pallet of sticks and skins or a modern queen-size four-poster, your body rejuvenates on the bed while your consciousness takes flight into the atmosphere of the eternal.

In your bed, you share the nighttime history of humankind, every time you lie down. Note the materials in your bed: the frame (metal or wood?), the mattress and box spring, the headboard, and the bedclothes. The goal is to go with woods and natural fibers. A simple spread and pillow may be fine for one person, while a comforter, duvet, several pillows, and bolsters are perfect for another.

Moran recommends "a mattress made from natural, breathable organic materials. An ideal combination is an organic cotton cover over dust mite–resistant wool batting and 100 percent natural latex. If you're not ready to buy a new mattress, consider a topper of pesticide-free wool covered with green cotton (green cotton is undyed, unbleached, and untreated) or organic cotton." If clearing out toxic materials is prohibitively costly, take steps slowly, over time.

Now take note of the other large objects in the room: dressers, chests, chairs, and other seating. Assess the smaller objects you have no doubt taken for granted over the years. For some, the dresser and chest of drawers are impersonal and utilitarian. For others, however, the bedroom is a private museum containing precious hand-me-downs from

Bed is a medicine.

～ A proverb

Oh sleep!
it is a gentle thing,
Beloved from
pole to pole.

❧ Samuel Taylor Coleridge,
*The Rime of the
Ancient Mariner*

parents or grandparents. Perhaps they are valuable antiques or just mismatched items from a secondhand store. You may display personal keepsakes there: Dad's old cuff links or Mom's faded sewing box. You may have private photos or handpicked artworks for "your eyes only." Decide whether an item holds personal meaning, some association that resonates in your heart. Move store receipts to the office and spare change to a drawer. Display the pebble you picked up while on vacation, but try to hide from view items of grooming (brushes, combs, cologne, et cetera).

Try to include only bedroom furniture that is needed and choose styles and placements that are harmonious with the position of the bed. Depending on available space, you can incorporate dressers, nightstands, a chest, chairs, a small desk or writing table, an armoire, a love seat or couch into your floor plan. However, as we shall see in the next section, less is more, where the bedroom is concerned.

What will you hang on the walls? You may include images of sacred places, saints, and prophets. Family photos also work well in a sacred space. After all, anyone you include in your prayers deserves to share your personal sanctuary. Frames should be of wood rather than metal or plastic. Art depicting beautiful, restful themes or places can work, in fact any image that conveys beauty or restfulness. Provocative imagery of commercial personalities, themes, or slogans, jagged or violent images, or secular messages should be removed. The most important consideration is that you choose each object, color, and fabric with intent. Welcome each piece and place it deliberately to become part of the overall sacred space.

Now that you have taken stock of your bedroom and improved its materials and furnishings, we will apply the ancient Chinese art of feng shui to maximize the influence of *ch'i,* a powerful hidden energy that permeates the universe.

BOUDOIR FENG SHUI

If the bedroom were merely a health-promoting compartment for a bed, our work would be done. But we are building the sacred bedroom from the ground up: this means that, with the materials and furnishings now carefully chosen, we are going to arrange the room in a way that transforms its very energy for maximum harmony and restfulness.

A hidden energy force, called *ch'i* ("chee") in Chinese, flows throughout the universe, through all spaces, around objects, and across landscapes. This concept corresponds with unified field theory and the "superluminal connectedness" of all things that physicists suggest exists beyond the reach of the senses. This force, however, has been known for over 5,000 years in many of the world's ancient traditions. The Hindus call it by its Sanskrit name, *prana.* The Jewish tradition calls it *ruach,* or "vital energy." It is called *spiritus* in Latin, *pneuma* in Greek, and *ki* in Japanese.

Ch'i is the Chinese word for "cosmic breath" and it is the underlying force of life. "Ch'i is the vital force that breathes life into animals and vegetation, inflates the earth to form mountains, and carries water through the earth's ducts," writes Sarah Rossbach in *Feng Shui: The Chinese Art of Placement.* "Ch'i is a life essence, a motivating force. It animates all things." *Ch'i* links spirit with substance. We have our own *ch'i.* The *ch'i* of our bodies and minds is affected by the *ch'i* of our surroundings.

Have you ever noticed how you are affected by where you are? It happens to everyone. You will be in a certain country, building, a room, or a place outdoors, and not feel right. You only feel better when you leave that place. In other places you feel inexplicably happy or comfortable. These differences in how you feel are determined by the quality of the *ch'i* in that place.

The flow of *ch'i* in your house and its rooms determines how it "feels" to be there, and your bedroom is no exception. Moreover, the quality of the *ch'i* flow can be improved or impaired by how objects are placed in the bedroom, especially the bed. To determine the best positions for these objects, we will use feng shui, the ancient Chinese art of placement.

Feng shui, literally "wind-water," is based on the principles of Taoism, which is the pre-Buddhist foundation of Chinese culture: its music, cooking, drama, medicine, and art. Taoist philosophy, set forth in the *Tao Te Ching* ("Classic of the Way of Power") by the sixth-century B.C.E. sage Lao-tzu, maintains that all that exists,

The Chinese believe the shape of a bed can mold a marriage. A bed with rounded corners can take the edges off of a rocky marriage. A large mattress is better than two twin-size mattresses lying side by side.

~ Sarah Rossbach,
*Feng Shui:
The Chinese Art
of Placement*

whether of matter, thought, or spirit, is one in a common field of unity. All manifestations — events, processes, changes — whether in the world or in your mind, are merely examples of this unity in which everything shares. The art of feng shui maintains that our moods contribute to the feel of our surroundings, and that our surroundings affect our moods.

Like other ancient arts, feng shui is complex and requires study to learn. Only the basics are presented here to give you a sense of some of the rules and guidelines that apply to a sacred bedroom. If you can afford it, engage a feng shui practitioner to guide you. You can also consult a host of fine books on the subject to deepen your knowledge. Some titles are included in the Bibliography.

Feng shui can be used in the design and placement of cities, buildings, and houses. The problems of existing buildings and rooms can be "cured," or simple changes can be employed to achieve the most beneficial flow of *ch'i*. Think of *ch'i* as an imperceptible wind pouring in your front door, flowing through your home, curving around objects, racing down hallways, stopping where its path is blocked, or being stifled in areas of clutter. The *ch'i* flows out through the back of your house, mainly through the windows. In the bedroom, you ideally want the *ch'i* to flow quietly and smoothly, to facilitate peace and restfulness.

With feng shui, you can create remedies for the *ch'i* flow in your bedroom to activate benefits in various departments of your life, such as career or family. In *The Feng Shui of Love,* T. Raphael Simons writes, "Feng shui may be described as the art of arranging space in order to bring about desired changes in one's life and circumstances. It is based on a profound knowledge of the ways environmental and mental conditions affect one another."

Since your mood and attitude are affected by your surroundings, you can make changes in your life by changing your environment. Many people claim that the circumstances of their lives change as well, once the principles of feng shui have been employed.

Feng shui masters say that when objects in your house or in a room are placed for the desired flow of *ch'i*, a number of positive changes can occur:

> If you want your home to attract and hold love, begin by cultivating peace and harmony in yourself. If you set these conditions inwardly, eventually they will manifest outwardly.
>
> ∾ T. Raphael Simons,
> *The Feng Shui of Love*

- You feel better in your home.

- Your home feels good to people who visit.

- Health, prosperity, and other aspects of life can improve.

- Blocks to certain of life's benefits can be removed.

- Your life can attract benefits to the areas activated.

A home built from scratch with this ancient art and its principles in mind, preferably with a feng shui–aware architect, would be ideal. However, most of us have neither the time nor luxury to begin from scratch. Most of us are unable to undo floor plan problems by moving walls, doors, or windows to establish the most "auspicious" structure and layout. That is where the "cures" come into play, because for any flaw in a room, there are ways to compensate.

To the feng shui master, the most important places in the home are the front door (the mouth or entrance of *ch'i* into the home), the bed (place of rest), and the stove (the source of food). Some feng shui masters call the bedroom the most important room in the house because it is the focus of health, love, life, happiness, and rest.

The ideal bedroom should be a room toward the rear of the house, away from the public spaces and away from the front door. You can choose a room not typically thought of as a bedroom — a den or study. It would be a room that is flooded by the morning sun. The bed and other furnishings are placed in ways that neither block nor amplify *ch'i*: you want the benefits of *ch'i*, but you do not want your sleep disturbed by agitated *ch'i*. How the ideal is accomplished will be highly individualistic, depending on your floor plan, furnishings, and the problems that need to be cured.

The ideal layout of your bedroom and the positions of the furniture can be determined by using a *bagua* ("bah-gwah"), the eight-sided feng shui template used by feng shui masters for thousands of years to maximize the beneficial effects of *ch'i* in eight important departments of life: marriage, fame, wealth, family/health, knowledge, career, helpful people, and children. (See Figure 2.1.)

One good reason for using Feng Shui is to find ways that are safe and comforting to allow us to reconnect with our inner self so we are always able to go there to receive higher guidance and solace.

     Nancy SantoPietro,
*Feng Shui:
Harmony by Design*

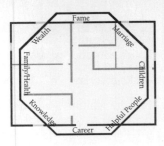

The Bagua

Figure 2.1

The *bagua* is a map of one's life condition. To use it, place it over a house or room floor plan, always with the Career sector over the entrance wall. (See inset.) By seeing how the rest of the floor plan falls under the *bagua,* the life condition can be determined and cures implemented where needed. If the house forms an L or some other non-four-sided shape, the missing or truncated sections will need to be cured: whatever sector falls in that incomplete corner indicates an incompleteness in your life. Extend the wall lines to complete a four-sided shape. At the incomplete corner of a house, plant a red maple tree, for example, or install a fountain to give life to that neglected segment.

In an L-shaped bedroom, shaped like a hatchet, place the bed in the larger portion of the L. Hang a small mirror in the smaller portion, as the reflection symbolically completes the missing corner. Be sure you cannot see your reflection in the mirror from the bed. You can also extend a divider to create a square or oblong room. In your room, as well as in your subconscious mind, completeness is achieved.

If you have a bathroom cutting into the position of Marriage, you may find yourself spinning your wheels in your relationships, or going through many relationships. This is because *ch'i* flows "down the drain" very quickly by way of the flowing water. Keep the bathroom door closed. If the bathroom creates an L, follow the instructions above. A laundry hamper in the Knowledge sector may have the effect of giving you diminished self-esteem about your education or knowledge.

Superimposing the *bagua* over your bedroom floor plan, you can interpret the strengths and weaknesses present in the arrangement of the room, the bed, and furniture. Wherever the bed is located will make that sector auspicious. The Marriage position is a good one for married people or someone who wishes to get married. The door should be visible from the bed, but the bed should not be directly opposite the door, as the *ch'i* is too strong for good rest. (See Figure 2.2.)

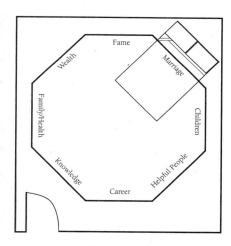

Figure 2.2

A bagua is placed over a bedroom floor plan.

The other departments of your life, particularly those that seem empty or neglected, can be activated or made auspicious by implementing cures. If you want to have children or to create auspicious conditions for your children, place a plant, altar, decorative lamp, or other item to activate that position of the room. The same is true for the Career area of the bedroom, the Wealth area, Family and Health, and so on.

One could debate the apparent elements of superstition or self-fulfilling wishes in this ancient art, but if you try to observe the principles of feng shui, the aura and happiness of your home will improve and be noticed by those who visit. My wife and I have made changes in our house and various factors, such as in the Wealth and Helpful People sectors, improved. We relocated the bed to the Fame position of the bedroom in the mid-1990s, and my wife's career as an author of cookbooks began in a big way.

Let's look at the bedroom and how to adjust the *ch'i* and implement cures for unavoidable problems.

What we think of as sacred actually is present in everything we do.

∽ **Riane Eisler**

PRACTICAL STEPS

Specific situations and problems can be cured according to the principles of feng shui.

Your bed deserves careful thought, because you spend as much as a third of your life there. Feng shui experts say not to buy the biggest bed of all, because then you can only reduce in size, meaning a divorce or lessening of energy, diminished quality of sleep, et cetera. If you live with a partner, be sure to share ideas together and come up with a layout that suits you both.

Depending on the shape of your room, try to follow feng shui guidelines for the bed and its placement. For example, the bed should not be placed in front of windows, because these are the portals through which *ch'i* exits the room. Your *ch'i*, effectively, could flow out the window with your dreams. In a four-sided room in which the door is near one of the corners, place the bed catercorner to the door so the occupant has a view of it — the room's mouth of *ch'i*. (See Figure 2.3.)

If the bed cannot be located in this spot, a small, octagon-shaped feng shui mirror can be placed on a wall to provide this view, as shown in Figure 2.4.

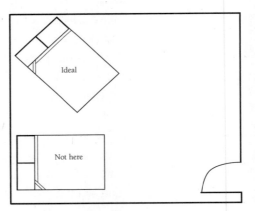

Figure 2.3

Mirrors should, how-ever, be avoided or used with care in the bedroom. They amplify *ch'i* and can energize the place of rest unnecessarily, working against your goal of calm relaxation. A boudoir mirror over the bed has been a naughty novelty for centuries, but the feng shui master will tell you that it symbolically introduces a third party to the relationship and may portend an affair on the part of one or both partners. Also avoid hanging a mirror opposite a window, as it overstimulates *ch'i*. Curtains can be used to mitigate this effect. A mirror hanging over your

Every person has a sage within his breast. It is just that people do not fully believe in this sage and bury it away.

     ❧ Wang Yang-ming, sixteenth-century Confucian sage

headboard can indicate heavy responsibilities and is, therefore, to be avoided. Finally, avoid placing a mirror so that the bed's occupant can see him- or herself. It is best to keep a mirror in an area for dressing, sequestered from the rest of the room even by a screen or a standing plant.

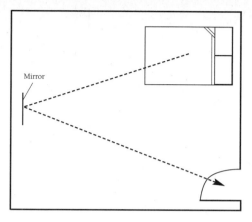

Figure 2.4

If the bed must be positioned beneath a beam, it may divide partners, literally "bisecting" their ideas and putting them at cross-purposes. In feng shui, such a problem is cured by hanging a flute (representing sound) from the beam. If the corner of a dresser unavoidably points at the bed, sit a trailing plant on the corner of the dresser so its branches spill over and hide that corner. A scarf can also be used for this purpose.

The cures offered by feng shui are not magical, but they have been used for thousands of years to enhance *ch'i* flow or slow it down, animate stagnant energy, or turn a harmful flow into a favorable one. They involve placing certain objects in strategic positions to counteract

Bed Placement and the Cardinal Directions

Bed Facing	Indication
North	Good for business
Northeast	Knowledge and learning
East	Rewarding family life
Southeast	Enhances prosperity
South	Can bring fame
Southwest	Happy marriage
West	Prominence for future children
Northwest	Good for travel

Bedtime Story

The Egyptians folded long linen sheets into thick pads and laid them on latticed beds where they used wooden headrests to keep their intricate hairstyles in place until morning. King Tut's all-wood royal bed was in the shape of two slender-legged cows connected by horizontal rails that were used by slaves to carry him about. He even gave audience from this movable bed.

some unavoidable inauspicious condition in the home or a particular room. (See "The Nine Basic Cures of Feng Shui" chart below.)

The Nine Basic Cures of Feng Shui

1. Lights/bright objects
2. Mirrors
3. Sound
4. Plants
5. Heavy objects
6. Color
7. Movement
8. Power/energy objects
9. Water

> A sacred place is anywhere you can be alone with your thoughts. It doesn't matter if you are in a crowd of people, in church or in a room by yourself.
>
> ✐ Susan Olsen

With these cures in mind, here are some bed-placement situations to avoid or cure if you cannot avoid them. Avoid placing the bed

- Where the foot points directly out the door in direct line with the incoming *ch'i*. If there is no choice, cure it by hanging a curtain, made from natural materials such as wooden beads, from the door frame. You can also hang a wind chime from the ceiling between the foot of the bed and the opening.

- Directly under a window or where the foot points out a window. Cover the window with curtains when sleeping so the *ch'i* is not rushing out past you.

- Under a sloping ceiling, eaves, or skylight.

- Against a wall, or where you can only get into or out of the bed on one side. (Sources differ on this point, so in this case go with your intuition and use one of the cures listed in the chart above.)

- Against a wall that abuts the bathroom or an elevator shaft. Flushing water and up-and-down motions occurring behind the sleeper's head can indicate instability or the loss of a relationship.

Be sure to place bureaus, chests, and armoires away from the foot of the bed, as they can cause an imbalance in the occupant's *ch'i*. Remember that the more clutter there is, the more restricted will be the flow of *ch'i*. Ideally your bed should have four legs so *ch'i* can freely circulate over and beneath it. Use a firmly attached headboard, which, it is said, helps to assure a stable relationship. If you live in a studio apartment or an efficiency, you need not abandon feng shui or these ideals of the perfect bedroom. The idea is to adapt them. Even if the foot of your bed is reachable from your eat-in kitchen, you can define small room areas within the room and then perform conscientious cures that give special energy to each of the eight sectors: place a plant at one virtual boundary, a small red object at another.

The key is to keep your attitude open to the sacredness of the space. I am inspired by the Jewish custom of affixing a mezuzah to the doorposts of a home and the principal rooms within it. A mezuzah (Hebrew for "doorpost") is a small rectangular box containing a tiny scroll upon which are written two verses from Deuteronomy (6:4–9 and 11:13–21) that include the words, "Hear, O Israel: The Lord our God is one Lord; and you shall love the Lord your God with all your heart, and with all your soul, and with all your might." Whatever your religion, choose a symbol that has deep personal meaning for you. Touch that symbol whenever you enter or leave your bedroom.

> I used to worship the Deity at the Kali Temple. It was suddenly revealed to me that everything is Pure Spirit. The utensils of worship, the altar, the door frame — all pure Spirit. Men, animals, and other living beings — all Pure Spirit. Like a madman I began to shower flowers in all directions. Whatever I saw I worshipped.
>
> ✍ Ramakrishna

Where Sheets Come From

For centuries, plain white linen sheets were the rule, mostly made at home by the homemaker until the 1920s and only becoming mass-produced in the 1930s. After the end of World War II, the Duchess of Windsor chose silk printed sheets from Porthault's linens in Paris and liked them so much she let them show. That began a fad for patterned sheets, which bailed out American mills, whose sales had dropped off due to the durability of white polyester and cotton blends. Famous designers were then hired to produce new patterns, and in the 1970s, 90 percent of all sheets sold were in blended prints and bright colors.

You can also add sacred meaning to the bed or sleeping area. Place a special spread on the bed; place the bed on an area rug; or pick out four little pillows for the corners of the bed: In this way, whenever you are there, you will always be aware of the sacred purposes you have begun to attribute to the bedroom.

With holistic redecorating and the energy enhanced through feng shui, we can now turn our attention to the idea of adding a spiritual practice to the bedroom.

THE ALTAR OF YOUR HEART

Humans have always sought ways to bring religious faith out of the abstract and into the tangible. We achieve focus for our beliefs by creating places for worship, prayer, and rituals. Experience proves that, without such practices, humans forget their beliefs and spiral into the existential without a lifeline. Your sacred bedroom provides a perfect sanctuary in which to create such a focus and maintain your faith, whatever it may be. You can accomplish this by constructing an altar — your personal display of symbols for what you hold sacred. An altar in your bedroom is a reminder of your faith and focus for your religious practices.

An altar is an honored display of images and objects used for worship, meditation, prayer, and ceremony. Altars have been used since as long ago as 8000 B.C.E., for everything from worship and sacrifice to giving thanks, honoring ancestors, and petitioning deities for blessings and favor. Altars can also be created to

- Honor specific aspects of the Godhead

- Invite fertility

- Promote success

- Ensure the safe return of a loved one

- Hasten recovery from illness.

"An altar, niche, or table in a place of solitude," writes architect Anthony Lawlor in *A Home for the Soul,* "can focus attention on objects and emblems that expand and deepen soul experience."

An altar is an outward display of what you hold dear in your heart of hearts — the place within you where you keep the prophets, teachers, people, places, and images that you have taken to heart since childhood. This inner sanctum within you, the holy place that you may not even be aware of, is where you truly live your beliefs, often at subconscious levels. In our bedrooms, altars can serve as sanctified settings where rituals and prayers are conducted, and where we can deliberately interact with the Divine. Because the bedroom space is protected from the mundane activities of the day, you can make the altar as personal as you like.

Altar Ideas

- Make your own candles.
- Prepare a scented bouquet.
- Make a dried flower display.
- Collect photos for a montage.
- Use an altar cloth of exotic material.

> The transformed place becomes our paradise as well, and in that world we're welcomed home.
>
> ～ Albert Pinkham Ryder, American painter

The concept of creating an altar is actually more familiar than you may realize. In *Altars: Bringing Sacred Shrines into Your Everyday Life,* author Denise Linn points out that we habitually create altars in our homes. "The urge to create sacred spaces is so deep in the human psyche that, even when there is no formalized intent to make an altar, we often create them subconsciously by the way that we carefully arrange objects on a desk or around a computer." Consider how we place treasured photos and objects on a piano or mantle. With the addition of a sacred intent, such as in the Shinto tradition of Japan, one could consider such a grouping a shrine to our ancestors.

The way we group and display objects in our homes is how we display that which we love. To include images and objects that are sacred to us in a special spot designated for worship — an altar — is simply taking what we love to the next step of deliberate intent.

We can, of course, practice our faith without the physical manifestation of an altar. However, an altar serves as a visual reminder to honor the Divine, and it can also invoke within us a sense of the sacred that truly belongs to us when we retire for the night and awaken in the morning. It is a beautiful focal point of what we hold sacred where we can sit unhurried, light a candle and a stick of incense, and make our faith active through prayer, worship, and personal rituals. (Chapter 4 will address prayer and meditation, and chapter 5 will explore ritual and ceremony in some detail.)

Making an altar in your bedroom, or anyplace else, should be thought of as a creative, personal process. Take your time with it. Plan it over several days — let the very process be part of your spiritual practice. You will want to select the location, the purpose, and the objects carefully. Pray for inspiration. Sit in your bedroom and contemplate every space. The perfect spot will reveal itself.

You can also use feng shui to locate your altar. Fit the *bagua* over your bedroom floor plan, placing, as always, the Career sector along the entrance wall. One approach to locating your altar is to use it as a cure for an unfortunate architectural feature, or for bringing auspicious energy to a missing corner, such as in an L-shaped room. If there are no floor plan problems needing a cure, then you can place the altar in any of the eight sectors that you would like to favor in your life. You can also place the altar directly opposite the foot of the bed, as my wife and I have done in our bedroom. Another approach is to place the altar against the east wall, aligned with the compass points, so when you face the altar you are facing the east, the direction of the eternal dawn and symbolic of Eden.

Your altar can be situated on a low or high table, desktop, dresser top, or on the floor of your bedroom. It can also be a room of its own, an attic dormer, or in the space under a stair. If you have only a little space available, you can create an altar simply by hanging a single religious symbol on the wall or placing it on the dresser. You can nestle a mini-altar on a shelf along a wall or in a corner with a corner shelf. You can also use a window ledge, a nook, or a closet as your altar space. Remember that your altar is a collection of symbols that, for you, evokes the most powerful feelings of your connection to the Divine, one that inspires you to think of spiritual matters, that comforts you, or gives you peace.

If you have very little space, you can create an altar on top of a single pedestal using miniature objects. Work with your space configuration, but don't be limited by it — improvise. If placed

Let all your things have their places. Let each part of your business have its time.

෴ Benjamin Franklin

Objects for the Altar

Use objects and images from the following list that have meaning for you:

Prophets, Saints, and Angels
Jesus
Buddha
Confucius
Shiva
Shakti
Kuan Yin
Mother Mary
Saints from your tradition
Archangels Michael, Gabriel, and others

Objects of Devotion
Prayer beads
Prayer flags
Religious books
Prayer wheel
Mandala
Chalice

Harvest Items
Flowers
Fresh fruit
Grain

Precious and Semiprecious Gems and Minerals
Diamond
Gold
Crystals

Aids for Prayer and Meditation
Incense
Bells
Chimes
Gong

A monk asked his teacher,
"What is enlightenment?"
The teacher responded,
"When I eat, I eat.
When I sleep, I sleep."

    恢 Ancient Zen tale

near a window, the arcing sun and moon add their ever-changing light to your altar setting.

If you do have the room for a tabletop altar, try to use natural materials. A wooden table, perhaps of fine wood, attractively turned and carved, would be ideal. Over the tabletop surface, place an altar cloth, preferably one of rich design and fabric, for this is the fabric of your life meshing with the fabric of universal consciousness. Choose colors according to your taste and décor. Be conscious of the materials you use: stone, glass, mineral, wood, or paper. Choose everything with a conscientious connection to the Divine.

Your altar should feature a dominant object as the central focus, with other objects placed around it: a picture of Christ, for example, a Star of David, or a statue of Buddha — whatever is sacred to you. If you have a personal teacher or guru, place his or her picture near that central focus. Add other images of saints or prophets who open your heart. Place an open holy book, such as the Bible, in front of the central figure, perhaps opened to a favorite passage. You can change the passage by day, week, or month, using it as a seed thought for meditation.

Next add some impersonal objects that can be used to facilitate your spiritual practice: an aromatherapy lamp and an incense burner, semiprecious gems or crystals. You can place a bell, cymbals, and candles on your altar. You can even include a little gong to start and finish a prayer or meditation session, sending your words into the universe borne on the eternal tone. Another idea is to burn a seven-day candle on your bedroom altar, organizing by day your spiritual rituals of prayer, meditation, and readings.

"Sacred diagrams, images, and icons can transport the mind from the harsh . . . to inner realms of subtlety and oneness," writes Lawlor in *A Home for the Soul.* For him, altars are "thresholds for reuniting with the lost powers of the soul and integrating them with the powers of thought and action."

In front of your altar, or nearby, keep a *zafu* ("cushion"), meditation bench, or a special chair that you will use only when meditating or praying. In that way, you can keep your altar space and its objects fixed in your mind for their sacred purposes.

Since my wife and I do not have room for a table in our bedroom,

Pray within thyself. Only first be thou a temple of God, because he in his temple will hear him that prayeth.

     St. Augustine

we have hung pictures of saints and teachers on the wall and surrounded them with a beautiful embroidered Tibetan prayer shawl. In the center is an image of Christ, and on either side are images of the Divine Mother. On a nearby dresser we have a tiny crystal goblet, symbol of the Holy Grail, an image of Buddha, an amethyst crystal cluster, and my wife's grandmother's rosary beads that she brought to this country from Hungary a century ago. To us, what is sacred transcends the confines of a single house of worship.

Whatever you place on your altar, it is important to realize that these objects have no power of their own. To attribute power to them regresses back to the days of fear, superstition, and idolatry that plagued most of the world's religions at one time or another. Simply allow yourself to respond inwardly to the icons, images, and symbols as they evoke feelings that are already within you. As Denise Linn says in *Altars,* an altar effects the way you feel. In a deep sense, "... it is the subconscious mind, which is the part of the brain that dictates our beliefs, that becomes profoundly imprinted with the symbolic meanings of the objects on an altar." We need these reminders in this distracting and demanding world.

The goal is to build an altar of the heart that represents your beliefs and displays symbols of what you hold sacred in your life. It should be comfortable for you. It is a tribute to what you and/or your partner worship in this most private room. Let worship come alive in the sacred bedroom, in the same place where you sleep and make love. Let your altar be part of a plan to enrich your night life with validation for your unity with life-giving Spirit.

Once you have completed your altar, the physical space of your sacred bedroom is complete. As time passes, you may make adjustments, additions, or even change the décor seasonally. In the meantime, you may care to conduct a ceremony to consecrate your altar, dedicating it to its sacred purpose, and then the sacred bedroom itself.

A Consecration for Your Altar

The altar should be consecrated because it holds the visual focus of the sacred in the bedroom. It displays the most precious symbols of your faith, the most powerful reminders of God within.

> Again and again look within thine own mind.
>
> ～ Padma-Sambhava

Use the traditions of your faith and its symbols to consecrate your altar. Light incense and your candles, then read or recite what, for you, expresses the following:

> In the name of I AM THAT I AM, I consecrate this altar, which contains the precious reminders of my faith and commitment to what I believe is right. Let this altar be an inspiration in my prayers and meditations. Let it shine for me as a reminder of the contents of my heart.

To close, ring the bell and let it resonate in the silence until the sound can no longer be heard. As the sound recedes, visualize the vibrations of the sound permeating every aspect of your sacred bedroom, all the way to the center of you — your heart. Of course, you may add a closing prayer as you wish.

A Consecration for Your Bedroom Space

Now, you may consecrate your bedroom for its sacred purpose. This step comes after you have completed your work with the space and arrangement of furnishings. Standing or sitting before your altar, extend your arms so as to embrace the room. With a deep breath, read or recite a consecration such as the following or one of your own creation:

> In the name of I AM THAT I AM, I consecrate this room as a sacred space for communing with the Divine through prayer, meditation, rest, sleep, dreams, and making love. In this space, I shall bring no disharmony in thought, word, or action. I ask the Highest Power to bless this space with healing and peace.

In Tibetan, Balinese, and certain indigenous American traditions, a space is cleared of past mental and emotional energy by way of "smudging," passing a smoking smudge stick through the space, allowing its smoke to cleanse the room's psychic quality. Smudge sticks are made of herbs that are twisted together, tied, and lit. The sticks can be purchased from meditation supply or health food stores. They must be made properly so they do not catch fire and are not overly smoky.

You can also cleanse the space with a bell, an incense stick, or

O! It's nice to get up in the morning, but it's nicer to stay in bed.

      Harry Lauder, Scottish singer

a small, tightly wound cloth onto which a few drops of lavender essential oil have been dropped. As you pass the smoke or fragrance through the space of the room, cover each of the eight corners, high near the ceiling and low near the floor, as *ch'i* can become stagnant in these areas. Use this method to cleanse the psychic space of a room, especially after an argument or some other disharmonious experience has taken place.

The important function of consecrating your space is to establish your intent and belief that you are in control of your space. Cleansing this space also helps you prepare to cleanse your inner space, your consciousness, your attitude, and to eliminate stress from the bedroom environment.

Recipes for the Sacred Bedroom

If you are having trouble falling asleep, try warm milk or a noncaffeinated, herbal tea before turning in.

Would you have a
settled head,
You must early
go to bed;
I tell you, and I
tell't again,
You must be in
bed at ten.

∽   Nicholas Culpeper

3

Sense
Education

The fullness of joy is to behold God in everything.

— Julian of Norwich

The sacred bedroom provides a quiet haven for contemplation. Let those who wish to grow there also redecorate the interior spaces of the mind. Refashioning your attitudes and freeing your heart from stress is the key. It will allow you to discover the richness of solitude and how to use the senses to experience the Divine more fully.

STRESS AND YOUR INNER SPACE

The newly rearranged bedroom welcomes you at day's end, its colors warm, its feng shui calming. The presence of an altar invokes feelings of a sacred space, and the bed is dressed decoratively, holding you safely for the night. This outer space of your personal sanctuary is prepared for sacred activities. It is time to prepare yourself — the sacred inner space of your psyche and the role of your attitude in making the bedroom a place for growth and healing.

Your body can be thought of as a temple that houses the soul, but your mind exists in the limitless space of consciousness — the I AM THAT I AM alive within you. Your inner space is the landscape of your soul, the realm of your thoughts and feelings. Your soul is that authentic self of your childhood, when you eagerly embraced and trusted the world as a safe, happy place. You still know this inner child's peace periodically. It emerges unexpectedly, such as when you are supremely relaxed before a mountain sunset or lounging in the company of someone you love. Perhaps you have known that place within in a moment's stillness after lovemaking, when everything was just right. Perhaps you have known it when deep in meditation or prayer, in the early morning hours after a sound sleep, before your day began, or late at night when the house was quiet.

As we grow up, this pure childlike consciousness becomes obscure and eventually forgotten amid the responsibilities and disappointments of our lives. That child is unable to live in our hearts because of our distrust of people and circumstances, dislike of ourselves, or because of fear. We draw close to that sacred space within when we receive a gift, a raise, or some other unexpected blessing that catches us off guard. On these occasions, we find ourselves momentarily as happy as a four year old, just before we snap back to our cautious, grown-up personas.

We can recapture that childhood innocence and gain access to our sacred inner space by choosing a new attitude and fueling it with the fire of our spiritual faith. We possess the higher knowledge that feelings of peace and love emanate from the Creator. We know that if we so choose we can radiate such qualities that project from God-Is-Love. The key is to cure our inner feng shui with a set of simple practices that I like to call spiritual arts: meditation, prayer, dream guidance, and training the senses. These tools are available to anyone who wants to strip away negative emotions, worry, and stress that block access to our sacred inner space. These tools, explained in this and the following chapter, will help you discipline your mind and claim your connection to the Divine in the sacred bedroom.

Keeping the effects of stress out of your bedroom is the first step. Your sacred bedroom space provides a private setting in

The knower of the mystery of sound knows the mystery of the whole universe.

∽ Hazrat Inayat Khan

which you can soothe the stresses of the day and spiritually recharge. We experience stress whenever we find ourselves in high-pressure conflicts for which simple solutions elude us. This often happens at work, where relationships with coworkers, the boss, or customers do not allow us to express our frustrations. Add a stressful situation with a partner or family members, and the effects of stress on the emotions and body are compounded. In addition to those outside pressures, we create our own stress: about our weight, appearance, habits, medical or legal problems, and even the lack of time to get everything done.

Stress builds up and causes a variety of debilitating medical and psychological conditions. It has been determined that as much as 50 to 80 percent of our modern illnesses are related to stress. Medications for stress are consumed regularly by as many as 40 million Americans, just to help them manage the symptoms of stress, which can include

> When things don't work well in the bedroom, they don't work well in the living room either.
>
> ∽ Dr. William H. Masters, Masters & Johnson Institute

- Exhaustion

- Anxiety

- Irritability

- Lack of motivation

- A weakened immune system

- Feeling old

- Feeling plain lousy

- High blood pressure

- Susceptibility to illness

Stress can hamper four of the bedroom's greatest purposes. It can prevent you from getting a good night's sleep, curtail your sex life, interfere with dreaming, and prevent the mind from relaxing and concentrating during meditation. These three activities are important to anyone's well-being, but they are essential if you want to enjoy the full benefits of your sacred bedroom.

One way to control stress and its effects is to more sharply focus your spiritual values. Train yourself to stop attaching your emotions to the mundane aspects of life: pressures of finance, relationships, time, and schedules. Learn to hold at a distance anything that is not welded to your core spiritual values, and stop investing your feelings in the trappings of the workaday world. You can learn do this over time and with practice, even if you are having partner problems, work for a difficult boss, or the collection agency is knocking at your door.

Begin to free yourself from stress by observing how you normally react to people, especially people who traditionally provoke in you a negative response, such as anger, resentment, or disgust. With practice, you can more objectively measure the things they say and do against the yardstick of your spiritual values. You can then deliberately choose not to buy into those words or actions. Even if they have adversely affected you, you can reason that if you allow them to cause you stress, you are allowing them to control your inner life as well as your outer life.

It is unfortunate that the bedroom can, itself, be a source of stress. The moral codes and medieval stigmas have certainly made their marks on our behavior. But the more telling causes of stress in the bedroom are the artificial expectations our society places on our physical appearance, relationships, and sexuality, resulting in widespread sexual frustration and dysfunction. The latter problems are beyond the scope of this book, but those who feel stressed can take advantage of the sacred bedroom by breaking some bad old bedroom habits.

Turning in: We often get into bed for the night preoccupied with the following day. Sometimes, we anticipate the next day with dread. When I was a child, I would become anxious on Sunday night because I knew the next time I awakened, I would have to go back to school. When you turn in, avoid thinking of sleep as merely a precursor to the following morning, but as an important event of its own that constitutes fully one-third of our lives. Think of the healthful rest it provides for body and mind and look forward to the schoolroom of your dreams.

Fear of being alone: We have seen how the presence of the Creator abides within us (in our hearts as love and in our consciousness as I AM THAT I AM awareness) and so, in that sense, we truly are never alone.

> None beholds him with the eyes, for he is without visible form. Yet in the heart is he revealed, through self-control and meditation. Those who know him become immortal. When all the senses are stilled, when the mind is at rest, when the intellect wavers not — then, say the wise, is reached the highest state. This calm of the senses and the mind has been defined as yoga. He who attains it is freed from illusion.
>
> ∽ Katha Upanishad

Sexual issues: If there are sexual issues from your past or between you and your current partner, find a way to not let them rob you of the restorative and healing dimensions of your sacred bedroom. Seek counseling for serious or chronic troubles, because a stressful bedroom time can impair good health. Use the "Spiritual Ideals Statement" described below, along with the meditation techniques described in chapter 4, to change your attitude and release negative feelings.

A powerful tool that can help you keep stress out of the bedroom is to write a Spiritual Ideals Statement, a personal mission statement that describes the highest purpose of your life and the rules you choose to live by. One could write pages about all the things one believes, but this statement should be brief, no more than a paragraph or two in length. Your spiritual ideals may be drawn from teachings of your chosen religion or from others, from ethical or moral laws, or even common sense wisdom. I hold that even atheists, if they are using a focused statement of their ideals, can control the effects of stress.

To build your Spiritual Ideals Statement, answer these five questions:

1. Is my soul eternal, created in the image of God?

2. Does my attitude determine how I respond to circumstances?

3. What are the basic spiritual laws I should live by?

4. What principles am I willing to commit to every day?

5. What are my long-term spiritual goals?

During the mid-1990s I lived for several years in a stressful environment that eroded my health. Listing my answers to questions such as these, I was able to sort out what was important in my life. I am not completely free from stress, but regardless of the pressures, I know my limits and have a brighter attitude about the changing circumstances of my life. The Spiritual Ideals Statement I try to live by reads as follows:

My consciousness is my soul and it will outlive my body.
The quality of my soul is shaped by my daily desires,

Bedtime Story

In Roman houses, the bedchamber was used for repose and eating, its tile floor leading through draperies to lovely gardens and countryside vistas. Roman citizens used hay, wool, and feathers to stuff sewn bags to make the first true mattresses. When Rome fell, the bed collapsed too, to Germanic tribes who preferred the old-fashioned ground. Europe slowly worked its way back to the latticed frame and rush mattress bed.

words, and actions. I try to observe the Ten Command-ments and think of others before I think of myself. I discipline my mind with meditation and keep my body healthy with yoga and a vegetarian diet. I shall endeavor to use my skills as a writer and editor to help change people's lives for the better.

I live my days confident that my Spiritual Ideals Statement rings true in my heart of hearts. It is logical and based on scriptural teachings that I respect. During the day, I try to measure the forces, actions, and words I encounter against the spirit of this statement, and, in that way, I take nothing to heart that does not conform to it. I try to perform my duties accordingly, whatever they may be. Whatever pressures, responsibilities, or mishaps that I cannot avoid, I do my best and come out the other side with my self-esteem intact and my body spared the ravages of stress.

Write a Spiritual Ideals Statement that suits you, your temperament, goals, and needs. Here are two more examples that you can use for inspiration when you write your own:

> I am worthy to be called a child of the Creator. I believe in the power of love and compassion and practice them every day. I dedicate my talents to creating good works in the world. Every day, I will spend time in prayer and meditation in order to renew my connection with the Creator.

> I believe I am eternal and that the distractions of this mundane world are only temporary. I honor my life by living in a clean environment, eating good food, and drinking good water. I uphold the tenets of [scripture of your choosing], and treat everyone as I wish to be treated.

The first night after you compose your Spiritual Ideals Statement, leave your stress and worries outside the bedroom door. If you are plagued by a relentless irritant, even a bedroom-related problem such as sexual dysfunction, think about it for a while before you retire for the night, but give yourself a time limit, say an hour before you go to bed. After the hour, write down the problem, in one sentence, and any possible solutions on a piece of paper or

---

We are of God.
That is what we are.
I saw no difference
between God and our
Substance but as if it
were all God.

∽ Julian of Norwich

in a journal before you enter your sacred bedroom: *Let the paper hold the problem and the stress for you until morning* — out there, in another room in the house. Protect your bedroom from rancor, ill feelings, and worries. Let this act create a vacuum in your mind in which the proper solution can appear.

This technique can work even if the source of your stress is the very partner you sleep with! If my wife and I are having an argument, we take a moment to center ourselves before entering the bedroom. If your spouse or partner does not appreciate the concept of a sacred bedroom, perhaps he or she will respect your choice, or maybe even come to embrace it over time. (Chapter 7 offers advice for those with spouses who do not embrace the concept of a sacred bedroom.) In the meantime, let the paper hold all the causes of your stress and enjoy the calm that comes with knowing that you are in control of your feelings.

Forming new habits is essential to adopting a new attitude. So, make up your mind never again to drag yourself to the bedroom unprepared for entering this sacred place. Never again bring with you the burdens of stress or snap off the lights besieged with worry. Think of the bedroom as an escape, that special place in which you can leave the outside world behind, including the nonbedroom spaces of your household. From now on, when you enter the bedroom, think of your presence there as a privilege. Enter the space that you have so carefully arranged and decorated, fully conscious of the new meaning you are giving to that space. Touch or acknowledge the religious symbols that you placed by the doorway to remind you that this is a place in which you can be your authentic self, commune with God, regenerate in sleep amid the pure energy of *ch'i*, and dream dreams that will help you get on in life.

You can become closer to your spiritual ideals, living stress free as that childlike authentic self, when you discover how to make the best use of the time you spend alone. This is part of a process of cleaning up the "room" of your consciousness, in the same way you cleaned up the space of your bedroom. The journey inward begins with you, and how you spend your time alone.

> The heart of the wise,
> like a mirror,
> should reflect all objects,
> without being
> sullied by any.
>
> ∾ Confucius,
> *Analects*

LOVE MY SOLITUDE

In ancient Benares, India, there was once a king. One night during the heat of midsummer, he went to an upper room of the palace and lay down on a couch laden with gold, silver, and precious stones. He had a servant girl massage him with a precious sandalwood ointment that was cooling to the skin. But the girl was wearing so many bracelets on her arms that they jangled noisily. Soon, the sound began to irritate him, so he asked the girl to remove one of the bracelets. She did as he asked, but there was only a little less jangling. He made her continue removing them until only one remained — then there was no jangling at all. Once the noise stopped the king had a sudden realization.

"This is what I will do with my kingdom and ministers! My subjects and attendants!" he proclaimed aloud. "This is what I will do with all my responsibilities." From that moment on, he was free from worldly desires. He spent the rest of his days in solitude, practicing meditation and prayer, and eventually became a solitary buddha (*pratyeka-buddha*).

Though most of us will never have the opportunity to give up an entire kingdom, we each need to spend enough time apart from our worldly desires to remind ourselves of what is truly important. We need a break from the assault of sights and sounds, information, blasting TVs, and beckoning computer screens. We need time away from the radio, the roar of traffic, the push and pull of conversations so we can become centered again. In constant company with partners, family, coworkers, friends, and acquaintances, we can go for years without being truly alone with our thoughts.

When we were children, we began to have conversations with ourselves. In those conversations, we decided who we were based on what we learned from parents and peers. We accepted certain descriptions of ourselves, lucky, happy, or funny, or negative attributes such as unworthy, stupid, or bad. We continue to have conversations with ourselves in adult life, but we often never finish them due to interruptions, responsibilities, entertainment, or the mind tracking on what's happening around us. As a result, we perpetuate a negative self-image based, in part, on unfinished thoughts.

Beauty is undoubtedly the signature of the Master to the work in which he has put his soul; it is the divine spirit manifested.

∽ Honoré de Balzac

Our conversations with self continue while we are driving, mowing the lawn, or doing the laundry. Sometimes we are lulled into daydreaming or woolgathering. We also continue the conversations as we are falling asleep, but they merely drift away as sleep overtakes us. Our thoughts may even cause a restless sleep. The fact is, most of this mental conversation is random, unstructured, and lacks purpose. We need to have complete conversations with self to help unravel the negative thinking and frenetic mental activity that steers us away from the authentic self. We need time alone in order to do this.

The time we spend in solitude can be used in a number of ways. Prayer and meditation are powerful tools to use during our alone time, and we will look at those in some detail in the next chapter. However, before you engage in prayer or meditation, you need to be aware of the importance of creating time alone for yourself. If you are unable to spend time in the woods, a park, on the beach, or elsewhere in the house, the bedroom is your prime venue, with the door closed, in which to enjoy some solitude. Plan some "downtime" in which to just sit and think; to do nothing, if you wish, mentally and physically, or to finish a conversation with yourself in which you can reassess your self-image, reconstruct a thought you had some time ago, or just get some rest. You can always sit by your altar and think, without involving formal prayer or meditation.

Whenever I am unable to spend time in nature, I spend it in my bedroom, seated in a comfortable chair, surrounded by the beautiful, inspiring objects that my wife and I have placed there. Sometimes I look out my window and just watch the birds and trees. I work out problems in my life or thinking, unrelated to job responsibilities or relationships, just enjoying the solitude of "being there," engaged in mindfulness of my place in the universe at that moment and nothing more.

If you share a bedroom with a partner, you may have to plan your moments of solitude. If your schedules place you in the bedroom at the same time every day, you may simply wish to take a walk and find somewhere you can be alone. This is especially true if your partner is unsympathetic to the idea of a sacred bedroom.

> Go sweep out the
> chamber of your heart.
> Make it ready
> for the dwelling place
> of the Beloved.
>
> ⟋ Mahmud Shabistri

A student asked his
meditation teacher,
"What is your
spiritual practice?"
The teacher responded,
"I chop wood and
carry water."

꙳ Ancient Zen tale

You will need to come up with creative solutions for solitude, meditation, and prayer, as well, and adapt.

Solitude is a healing, healthful activity that is perfectly suited to the bedroom. In solitude, you can claim your impressions, thoughts, and feelings as your own. Rejoice in this independence, and enjoy your communion with the I AM awareness as a personal triumph every time you are by yourself.

Solitude can help you redecorate the heart and give the mind a rest. In solitude, we can turn on our hearts with love and appreciate the bedroom as a place of freedom and healing. In our complex, distracting age, we need to take steps for getting back in touch with who we really are. Reducing stress is an important part of the sacred bedroom. Awakening our senses is another.

AWAKEN YOUR SENSES

On May 13, 1373, a thirty-year-old English woman lay on her deathbed wracked in pain, eager to die. But instead of dying, her pain miraculously lifted. Recovering completely from her illness, she experienced a series of sixteen mystical visions she would later call "showings," in which God, Christ, and Mary spoke to her.

Considered the first lady of English letters and England's greatest mystic, Julian of Norwich described these "showings" in *Revelations of Divine Love,* considered one of the most extraordinary and beautiful expressions of sacred experience.

Her experiences took place on three levels: spontaneous new understanding; visions of the spiritual entities that spoke to her; and "bodily visions," in which she was intensely aware through the senses of sight, hearing, and sometimes even smell. The sensual aspect of our humanness became a frequent theme in her fourteenth-century masterwork. "It is when our soul is breathed into our body," she wrote, "that we are made sensual," implying that our senses are natural and inseparable from our humanity. She explained this concept further, writing, "God is nearer to us than our own soul, because God is the ground in which our soul stands and God is the means whereby our Substance and our Sensuality are kept together so as to never be apart." That fact is, we underutilize the intelligence of our senses, and we neglect to use them as instruments in our spiritual life. We know that, when given too much emphasis, the senses can mislead and confuse us. However, this intelligence of the senses to perceive God was described in a tiny book published in the 1940s entitled *The Sanctity of the Senses* by Swami Premananda, who wrote, "All sense-powers are gifts of God to man that he may perceive the celestial glory of the phenomenal universe, manifest his own innate divine qualities, and gain the inner vision of his transcendental perfection."

Premananda believed that "not by the mortification of the senses, but by their proper and complete utilization, man fulfills the will of God on earth. The senses are not accidental adjuncts to man, they are the necessary instruments of soul that it may live, love, serve and unfold. God created the soul. Soul evolved the senses to consummate the purpose of its existence."

There is no more intimate place than the bedroom to release the power of your senses to make you aware of the sacred. Where but in this most private chamber can you open your senses to all the manifestations of divinity within us? Let's look at each of the five senses and the expanded role they can play in the sacred bedroom.

Sight

Harmonious surroundings not only please the eye but also have a direct bearing on your mood. The last chapter dealt with creating a bedroom space that was healthful and visually pleasing. Through the art of placement, you rearranged your bedroom and applied cures for the maximum flow of *ch'i*. You removed distractions, such as the TV, and placed sacred objects on your altar. You hung inspiring art or images on the walls and chose pleasing colors and fabrics.

Whenever you are in your sacred bedroom, remember to focus your awareness on the beauty you have created there. Spend a moment there in appreciation and gratitude every day. Regard your beautiful altar of sacred objects and images, the flowers, and decorations as healing and inspiring, if just by their beautiful appearance. Rejoice in the curving sway of a candle flame. Make

When oft upon my couch I lie,
In vacant or in pensive mood,
They flash upon that inward eye,
Which is the bliss of solitude.

ಅನ William Wordsworth

Beauty is merely the
Spiritual making itself
known sensuously.

∽ Hegel

changes in your bedroom or to your altar as you feel inspired
to do so. Behold your partner, too, as a manifestation of divine
beauty in your life.

The sense of vision also operates inwardly when we use the
power of visualization to create positive changes in our lives.
Visualization is a technique of mentally picturing a condition or
situation in order to help it manifest. Visualization instructs the
mind and awakens the heart to all possibilities. It helps remove
self-imposed obstacles, arising from negative thinking, and to
achieve your spiritual and material goals. Using a visual focus for
concentration and contemplation can also help you free your
mind from your problems and disperse disturbing thoughts and
memories. (See the accompanying "Visualization Exercise.")

Visualization Exercise

As you breathe deeply, visualize yourself surrounded by the shim-
mering light of God-Is-Love. In your imagination, picture the light
protecting, healing, and restoring your energy. Maintain the image
of the light around you for a full minute. Whenever you picture
yourself in the light, you reinforce a positive self-image in your subconscious mind. Apply this exercise to goals, too. Picture yourself
radiantly healthy, having the abundance you need to live your life,
happy among your friends, or ready to be a responsible partner in
a relationship. Use visualization with the meditation techniques
described in chapter 4.

Hearing

Everything in the universe vibrates. Ancient texts proposed
this and modern science has confirmed it. Patterns of vibration
manifest in the shrinking and expanding of the universe; in the
cycles of the seasons; phases of the moon; electrons beating
around a nucleus; the long cycles of planets in their orbits; the
spectrum of light waves; and the vibration of sound. All vibration
is one in the emanation of God-Is-Love.

All frequencies of all vibration mesh together into the single
Sanskrit syllable "om." The vibration of the universe is constant

and permeates everything, always. Zen monks, it is said, have achieved enlightenment by becoming one with sound, such as the sound of a waterfall. Religious traditions the world over feed the fires of faith with music: choruses united in song, the soulful swells of a pipe organ, and the intonation of bells.

The sounds we hear are only a tiny portion of the vast universe of vibration, yet every sound has a powerful effect upon us. The music we choose can be thought of as food: the food we eat with our ears. We can soothe the savage beasts of negative emotions with music.

Playing music in your sacred bedroom is not necessary. However, if you decide to do so, choose music that speaks to you, but that creates a calming, relaxing, meditative effect. The music you play should speak to you, and invite you to rejoice in its beauty.

Choose music to accompany specific purposes:

- *Meditation:* Harp music; Japanese, Indian, or Native American flute music; Tibetan bells.

- *Lovemaking:* Any of the above, along with light classical or romantic-period music, something that elevates your feelings or that enhances your sexuality.

- *Prayer:* Use recordings of chant or the sacred music of any land.

- *Cleaning:* Use music that you find relaxing and healing as a background. As you clean, be mindful of its healing effect and your purpose in playing it.

Try to use ethereal instrumental music in your bedroom, as nonprayer lyrics can distract more elegant thoughts. Remember, too, that part of our appreciation of sound is recognizing the power of silence. You can feel silence just as you can feel the tones, phrasing, and dynamics of music. Listen deeply in the silence, for behind that silence is the primal sound of oneness binding Creator and creation.

Whether or not you employ music in your bedroom, try to use the pure tone of a bell, cymbal, or tiny gong to open and close prayers or meditation sessions. By the purity of their tones, they

He that has known the glory of the self within the ephemeral body — that stumbling block to enlightenment — knows that the Self is one with Brahman, Lord and creator of all.

∽ Brihadaranyaka Upanishad

evoke the vibration of the word "om." You may also ring a tone at the beginning and ending of lovemaking. For added atmosphere in your sacred bedroom, hang a wind chime outside your window.

During the day, even away from home, listen with focused awareness to the sounds around you and try to think of every sound as a component of "om." Learn to listen within to the answers from your heart of hearts, the I AM THAT I AM that is part of you.

Touch

In 1887, twenty-year-old Annie Sullivan discovered that the only way she could teach a child named Helen Keller, who could neither see, hear, nor speak, was through the sense of touch. Through touch alone, she guided Keller not only to communicate from her dark and silent world, but on to graduate with honors from Radcliffe College.

We are not so familiar with communication by touch outside of intimate relationships, nor are we often encouraged to appreciate the power of touch to convey love. In many other parts of the world, touch is natural, expected, proper, and accepted. In France, Italy, and other parts of Europe men and women greet each other with an embrace and kisses upon each other's cheeks. In the Middle East, men can be seen holding hands as they walk and talk. Not so in the United States, where public touching is often limited to a handshake or an embrace between female friends. Touching is practiced only to varying degrees even among family members here.

The sense of touch is perceived by the brain when electrical messages are sent by nerve endings in the skin from even the slightest contact. Touch precedes all the other senses, as it is the most basic form of communication — the first we encounter after we are born. Deprivation of touch in infancy has been linked to various degrees of physical and mental handicaps and psychosomatic illnesses later in life. Touch deprivation is most devastating in emotional terms, as people so deprived grow up unable to feel deep emotions and receive or express love. Children who are touched and held often grow up to be more outgoing and to feel good about themselves.

You are the temple
of God.

~ I Corinthians 3:16

A hug or reassuring squeeze of the shoulder can be healing for someone who — and there are millions of them — endure years without so much as the contact of a handshake with another human being. Many people never receive another loving touch after their mother touched them in childhood — in their bedroom.

Our expressions of love are restricted in public, but not so in the home. In the bedroom, we are free to express love in every way, except when our personal inhibitions prevent us. We can use touch in the bedroom in many ways to heighten our sense of connectedness to the sacred within us, to our partners, and even to the objects we have placed there.

Here are some practices and activities that can be used to enhance your appreciation of touch in the sacred bedroom. The first suggestion can be practiced by an individual and those that follow are for partners to practice together:

- *In touch with your room:* If you have chosen the objects for your sacred bedroom carefully, they will not only be pleasing to the eye, but of natural materials that feel good to the touch. Deliberately touch the fabrics, sacred objects, and wood in your bedroom, and appreciate how they feel on your fingertips, against your cheek, or upon your lips.

- *Back rubs:* Nothing beats a good back scratch or rhythmic kneading of neck and shoulder muscles. Partners should give equal time to each other, say right before bed or upon waking in the morning.

- *Touch exercises:* Face each other while seated on the floor or in chairs. Place your palms together and gaze into each other's eyes. Try to convey your love through eyes and hands alone. Observe how much easier it is to be honest through your hands; how touch helps your fears, selfishness, and pretenses drift away.

- *Cuddling:* When was the last time you simply cuddled with your partner? Try it without speaking and not as a prelude to sex. Let your ability to communicate through touch expand and grow. It's all right if power cuddling sets you laughing.

I shut my eyes
in order to see.

❧ Paul Gauguin

Weariness can snore
upon the flint
When resty sloth finds
the down pillow hard.

∽ Shakespeare,
Cymbeline

• *Massage:* Once a month, if not once a week, partners should give each other an hour of massage. Light a candle and some incense; play soft instrumental music. Use an aromatic oil (see the "Aromatherapy" section later in this chapter) and rub it into the skin in long smooth strokes. Knead and relax tight muscles. Work down to the connective tissues for that ahh! of ultimate relaxation. Take a class together at a local massage school. If you live without a partner, you can learn to apply many self-massage techniques.

Taste

In *The Sacred Kitchen,* coauthored with my wife, Robin Robertson, we explored many aspects of food, its connection to the Divine, its *ch'i* energy, and the role food plays in spiritual ritual and ceremony the world over. The sense of taste is particularly applicable in the bedroom, whether you offer fruit on your altar, share fresh strawberries with your partner, or simply enjoy breakfast in bed or a midnight snack.

Recipes for the Sacred Bedroom

Midnight Snacks: Why not replace your childhood favorite, cookies and milk, with a more healthful alternative? Consider a small bunch of sweet, seedless grapes or other fresh fruit that will be refreshing, satisfying, and easy to digest. Or try a soothing cup of herbal tea or vegetable broth — even better for digestion.

We tend to be pickier concerning taste than about our visual surroundings, music, or scent, seldom thinking of taste as an extension of our connection to the Creator.

Science tells us that taste buds are clusters of chemically receptive cells located on the surface of the tongue that detect sweet, salty, sour, and bitter. Receptor cells in the soft palate and in the throat pick up sour and bitter. In fact, the overall experience of flavor is a combination of taste, smell, and touch. Eating actually uses all the senses, as our enjoyment of food includes its appearance, how it feels on the lips and tongue, its texture as we bite into it, and possibly even the sound of its crunch.

The association of taste with sensory pleasure is well known. In the sacred bedroom, as well as wherever you eat, take time to appreciate the appearance, flavors, and textures of the food — whether it is a morsel used as part of a prayer ritual, eating the fruit that had been offered on your altar, or a bedtime snack shared with your partner — as further proof of the infinite variety the Creator has provided on the earth. When you are away from the bedroom, try to heighten your awareness of flavors. For example, focus your attention on the coolness of mint, the sting of hot pepper, the warmth of cloves, or the astringency of an orange. Let the sense of taste be one more way to celebrate your connection to the Divine in your sacred bedroom.

Smell

The power of scent to alter moods, improve attitude, and implement fragrance-related remedies for a host of physical and emotional afflictions has been known for thousands of years, in and out of the bedroom. It may surprise you to know that the sense of smell is more powerful than all the others — directly linked to your moods and memories of events many years past.

A smell can snap you back in time to the moment and feelings of an experience in the past. The circumstances, people, situation, even the weather can come back to you. In the bedroom, smells become powerful reminders of your partner, in particular of lovemaking. Fragrances can stimulate feelings of affection or even sexual arousal. The fragrance of a partner's hair or cologne can not only linger in the nostrils long after lovemaking, but actually stimulate sexual feelings when that smell is encountered in another place and situation.

The modern art and science of aromatherapy (see the "Aromatherapy" section below) began in the late 1920s under the hand of French chemist René-Maurice Gattefossé and expanded in many places in Europe during the 1960s. A study at the University of Wisconsin in 1986 by Arch Minchin, Ph.D., proved that fragrances can change moods and energy levels.

> The best and most beautiful things in the world cannot be seen or even touched They must be felt with the heart.
>
> ✐ Helen Keller

These roses under my
window make no
reference to former
roses or to better ones,
they are what they are;
they exist with
God today.

∽ Ralph Waldo Emerson

When a fragrance is smelled, aroma molecules from the substance affect the brain. The molecules are detected by sense receptor cells in the nose, which cause enzyme and electrical activity in the olfactory bulb. The olfactory bulb is part of the limbic system of the brain, the network of subcortical organs where our emotions, motivations, sexuality, and learning operate. The limbic system is the crossroad between the left and right hemispheres of the brain as well as the voluntary and involuntary nervous systems. Aromatherapy uses specific aromas to stimulate these systems to react, often subconsciously, to produce desired effects.

It is not clearly known how molecules of essential oils affect the emotions, but some of the effects routinely observed by aromatherapists include improving health, relieving anxiety, stress, and fear, and bringing into the consciousness more confidence and enhancements to various areas of your life, such as your love life. In the sacred bedroom, scent can be used effectively for pleasure, healing, and even to induce sleep and enhance rest or meditation.

In the sacred bedroom we can be especially creative with the sense of smell through the art of aromatherapy, which deserves a section all its own.

AROMATHERAPY

You are a complex sentient being with needs, desires, strengths, weaknesses, and a complement of senses that often drive your moods and attitudes. As mentioned above, smell is linked to memory and can be used to alter your mood and enhance your experiences in the sacred bedroom through aromatherapy.

The ancient practice of aromatherapy applies scents for specific uses, ranging from restoring health to curing depression, altering moods, and improving your love life and relationships. Aromatherapists ply their craft through the use of aromatic essential oils — highly concentrated essences of plants, flowers, barks, herbs, leaves, roots, resins, and spices. Extracted through various processes, the essential oils — more the consistency of water than of a true oil — contain up to seventy times the concentration of the individual source plant. Drops of the essences, alone or in combination with others, are used in various ways on the body, in massage oil, or in the air through diffusion.

Essential oils can be used in the bedroom to produce various effects that can enhance your success of making the bedroom a sacred place of healing, restoration, relaxation, sleep, worship, and lovemaking. Fortunately, there are scores of essential oils and combinations that can be effectively used in the bedroom.

The essences enter the body by absorption into the skin and around the hair follicles in the case of massages and baths, and into the nasal and respiratory mucous membranes and lungs and surface capillaries in the nose when inhaled.

As many as 3,000 essential oils are used throughout the world, although many of them are only used in their areas of origin. Most authorities agree, however, that there are between 30 and 60 basic oils that would suffice for a starter aromatherapy kit for home use. Listed below are 32 essential oils from which recipes for your sacred bedroom can be made. (Oils used in the recipes in this chapter are marked with an asterisk. Sources for essential oils are listed in the "Resource Directory" at the end of the book.)

*Basil: Soothes the nerves, stimulates clarity of thought and decision making. Relieves mental exhaustion, negativity, and fatigue.

*Bergamot: Uplifts feelings and brings joy. Relieves depression, anxiety, apathy, and nervous tension.

*Cedarwood: Helps release anxieties while promoting relaxation, regeneration, and longevity. Promotes concentration, persistence, and a feeling of nobility. Reduces stress.

Chamomile (German): Calms, comforts, induces understanding and a deep sleep. Fights nervousness, frustration, irritability.

Chamomile (Roman): Calms and eases the emotions, mind, and body. Induces sleep; promotes spirituality. Similar in effect to lavender.

Cinnamon: Encourages warmth, steadfastness, benevolence, and directness in communication, while reducing instability, severity, malice, and superficiality.

Bedtime Story

By the fourteenth century, wealthy English persons slept nude under blankets and embroidered, gem-bordered sheets. The poor covered themselves with wool or skins. The Crusaders brought back the idea of the double bed from the East, but knights often slept sitting up against pillows, their swords at the ready. Sometimes a bed was surrounded by protective wood paneling. Canopies, originally designed to keep out water and bugs, rose above beds; lamps hung within and they, together with the cross-shaped design of a sword's handle, kept away the devil. Beds were big, six feet by seven feet, but bigger beds were coming — a result of peaceful times.

At the time of
night-prayer,
As the sun slides down,
The route the senses
walk on closes,
The route to
the invisible opens.

꙰ Rumi

*Clary sage: Acts as a euphoric for the chronically depressed; relieves stress and depressive thought patterns. Promotes confidence, communication, and groundedness.

Cypress: Promotes inner strength, wisdom, and self-control. Relieves nervous tension, anxiety, and a weak will.

Eucalyptus: Cleanses the mind and body. Invigorates, energizes, clears the thoughts. Defuses heated emotions, mood swings, and tantrums.

Fennel: Promotes enlightenment and has a warming effect on the emotions. Relieves mental and emotional blocks, boredom, and loss of creativity.

*Frankincense: Aids meditation and is excellent for use on the altar. Disperses fear and comforts the mind. Helps overcome attachments.

*Geranium: Helps balance mood, emotional highs and lows. Relieves tension.

Ginger: Strengthens and encourages. Boosts confidence, warmth, and empathy. Helps to counteract sexual anxieties and sadness.

Jasmine: Acts as a euphoric for sensuality, sexuality, calm relaxation, optimism, and inspiration. Counteracts depression, pessimism, and low self-esteem.

*Juniper: Aids spiritual and meditative states. Clears the mind of undesirable emotions. Reduces melancholia, weeping, and guilt.

*Lavender: This great calming and soothing aroma balances emotions, nurtures, and gently sedates. Inspires compassion as it fights irritability, fear, nightmares, moodiness, and burnout.

*Lemon: Uplifts the spirit, cleanses the mind, enhances alertness and clear thinking. Relieves resentment, bitterness, touchiness, and a bad attitude.

*Myrrh: Stimulates courage and gives support for taxing emotional demands. Rejuvenates, inspires, helps to focus life's direction.

Narcissus: Mesmerizes, inspires, and enhances creativity and inner vision. Calms nervousness, weakens addictions, dispels illusions.

*Neroli: Induces spirituality. Reduces anxiety in stressful situations, relieves worry. Arouses. Relieves shock, panic, hopelessness.

*Orange: Refreshes and energizes; promotes communication and enthusiasm. Relieves selfishness, obsessions, and withdrawal.

*Patchouli: A reputed aphrodisiac (increased with use of ylang-ylang), it relieves anxiety and uplifts the mood. Battles sluggishness and lethargy.

Peppermint: Wakes the mind, stimulates the brain, and enhances clear thinking. Emotionally refreshes and relieves mental fatigue.

*Pine: Refreshes and inspires. Helps to clear the mind. Promotes humility, forgiveness, sharing, while relieving guilt, shame, regret, and self-blame.

*Rose maroc: Encourages passion, inner vitality, freedom, and sensuality. Combats grief, fears of sexuality, love, and letting go.

Rose otto: A euphoric that nurtures, heals emotional wounds, comforts, rejuvenates, and stabilizes the emotions. An antidepressant and fertility enhancer.

*Rosemary: Confers vigor, strength, and centering. Heightens sensory perception and sharpens the memory. Relieves memory loss, learning problems, and indecision.

Sage: Cleanses the thoughts and calms. Stimulates and refreshes. Enhances mental clarity and sense of purpose.

*Sandalwood: An aphrodisiac that enlightens, promotes spiritual, and meditative states. Can relieve irrational fears and stimulate courage and wisdom. Adds stability during major changes in life.

Thyme linalol: Motivates, energizes, and gives courage. Helps fight lack of direction and blockages.

*Vetiver: Grounds; lends spiritual calmness. Fortifies as it diffuses anger. Said to promote abundant finances. Attracts opportunities. Relieves anxiety and emotional burnout.

*Ylang-ylang: Dispels anger at oneself and other people. An aphrodisiac that warms with sensual awareness. Sensual. Relieves depression, soothes the nerves.

The substance of the universe is in us; the one force, energy, sustains that substance, and that substance of the universe is our consciousness.

— Antony Andreasen

I shall light a candle of understanding in thy heart, which shall not be put out.

✍ Apocrypha,
2 Esdras 14:25

Essential oils have been used for centuries to make pomanders, potpourri, creams, mist sprays, baths, and body powders. Cleopatra soaked the sails of her vessels in rosewater so Marc Antony would know of her approach. Queen Victoria made lavender a household word.

Essential Oil Dos and Don'ts

- Essential oils must be diluted in a carrier oil before applying them to the skin because they are highly concentrated and can be toxic.
- If sensitivity to the skin results, soothe the skin immediately with pure carrier oil and then wash the area with soap and water. Use weaker solutions of the desired oil, or do not use it.
- Pregnant women should consult an aromatherapy authority before using essential oils, since they can stimulate the uterus.
- Avoid getting oils or sprays in the eyes.
- Never drink essential oils.
- Keep essential oils out of the reach of children.
- People with allergies should consult a physician before using essential oils.
- Do not use essential oils if you are using medications, recreational drugs, or alcohol.

You can use essential oils in the bedroom in a number of ways. Use them to set a mood for lovemaking, a sacred atmosphere for meditation, or an aura in the room for a relaxed sleep. You can use fragrances to help you overcome negative emotions or mental preoccupations during the night. They are fun to use and experiment with.

Essential oils are highly concentrated and most commonly diluted in a vegetable-derived carrier oil, such as olive, sunflower, safflower, or almond, according to the suggestions below. (Cold-pressed oils are preferable because they do not contain processing chemicals.) Avoid applying oils full strength since they can irritate and damage the skin. Never use them in or near the eyes. Some essential oils can be toxic and should never be consumed without first consulting a professional aromatherapist.

Essential oils can be used to good effect with several simple devices that diffuse their fragrances into the air (see the "Resource Directory" at the end of the book):

- *Aroma lamps or burners:* A small bowl of water mounted on a ceramic or metal stand under which is placed a small candle or electric bulb. Essential oils are added to the water and the heat releases the scent. The heat disperses the aroma into your room and you can begin enjoying the effects of the fragrance within minutes. Be careful not to spill essential oil onto lightbulbs or flames: They are flammable. Also called a "diffuser." (Use six to twelve drops.)

- *Candles:* Essential oils can be used with candles by placing a drop of oil into the wax once it has begun to soften. (Use caution: Keep the bottle away from the flame as it may be combustible.)

- *Lightbulb ring:* This refers to a ceramic or metal attachment that uses the heat of the lightbulb to convey the scent of essential oils throughout a room. The oil should be placed in the ring before setting the ring on the bulb. (Use one to two drops at a time.)

- *Mister or sprayer:* Use a product made for this purpose or any household plant sprayer or misting bottle that has first been thoroughly cleaned inside. Combine very warm water with essential oil and spray into the air to lightly scent a room. (Use six drops per cup of water.)

- *Bowl of water:* Combine boiling water and a few drops of essential oil in a heat-proof bowl to release the scent.

Following are instructions on how to mix essential oils to create blends, dilutions, and massage oils.

Pure essential oils and blends: You can create a concentrated, undiluted essential oil blend by simply dropping the desired oils

Measurements

100 drops = 1 teaspoon
300 drops = 1 tablespoon
1 teaspoon = $1/3$ tablespoon
1 tablespoon = $1/2$ fluid ounce

full strength into a $1/4$-ounce brown glass bottle, then rolling and turning the bottle in your hands and allowing it time to blend. Use concentrated single oils and blends sparingly; for example, one drop to scent a handkerchief draped over a lampshade or one to two drops in a lightbulb ring. Add pure oils to the water of an aroma lamp or burner.

Essential oil dilution: Use diluted essential oils for application directly to the body. Drop oils into a $1/2$-ounce glass bottle according to the desired recipe, then fill the bottle to the shoulder with the carrier oil. Roll and turn the bottle in your hands and allow time to blend. Diluted oils are used as perfumes, rubbed onto the skin for healing effects, and to make massage oils.

Massage oil: Make a massage oil by mixing 1 or 2 ounces of carrier oil with the required drops of essential oil or oil blend in a $2 1/2$- to 4-ounce brown glass bottle. Use 12 to 15 drops of a pure or blended essential oil per 1 ounce of the carrier oil. Use as much as 25 drops in 2 ounces of carrier oil. Because essential oils can be expensive, you may desire to make such small quantities of massage oil for each use. Mix the ingredients by rolling and turning the bottle in your hands. Wait several hours for the oils to mingle.

For the best effect, purchase only pure essential oils and unrefined carrier oils. Their effects will be more noticeable because they are purer and have stronger *ch'i*. Avoid using oils that have been solvent extracted or that are synthetic or processed. The oils you purchase and the blends you make from them should be stored in sealed brown glass bottles, since their effectiveness is diminished by light. Brown glass bottles also preserve the oil's *ch'i*. Store them in a cool, dark place away from the sight or reach of children.

The following recipes can be used effectively in a sacred bedroom. They are organized by purpose, but feel free to experiment on your own or consult an aromatherapy authority to investigate the use of essential oils for physical health.

> Both religion and sexuality heal the split between ourselves and the universe. We discover that we are indeed "part of everything" and one with the mystery of life. To talk about God in relation to our sexuality means to be aware of love moving in us, for "in God we live and move and have our being."
>
> ‿ Dorothee Soelle, theologian

AROMATHERAPY RECIPES FOR A SACRED BEDROOM

Calm and Serenity
Lavender — 5 drops
Orange — 3 drops
Patchouli — 3 drops

The Sacred Bedroom Blend
Clary sage — 4 drops
Patchouli — 4 drops
Rose — 4 drops
Sandalwood — 4 drops
Ylang-ylang — 4 drops

Aphrodisiac pour Mademoiselle
Bergamot — 5 drops
Sandalwood — 5 drops
Ylang-ylang — 5 drops

Aphrodisiac pour Monsieur
Clary sage — 2 drops
Orange — 5 drops
Patchouli — 3 drops
Ylang-ylang — 3 drops

Rest
Bergamot — 4 drops
Frankincense — 5 drops
Vetiver — 5 drops

Stress
Cedarwood — 3 drops
Lavender — 4 drops
Neroli — 3 drops

Relaxation
Bergamot — 3 drops
Cedarwood — 4 drops
Lavender — 3 drops

Sensory Awakening
Clary sage — 5 drops
Geranium — 5 drops
Orange — 10 drops

Morning Arise
Lemon — 3 drops
Pine — 6 drops
Rosemary — 5 drops

Anxiety
Bergamot — 5 drops
Cedarwood — 5 drops
Lavender — 3 drops

Nervousness
Basil — 4 drops
Bergamot — 10 drops
Lavender — 8 drops

What lies behind us and what lies before us are tiny matters compared to what lies within us.

∾ Ralph Waldo Emerson

Confidence
Cedarwood — 5 drops
Frankincense — 4 drops
Sandalwood — 4 drops
Vetiver — 4 drops

Meditation #1
Bergamot — 4 drops
Frankincense — 6 drops
Myrrh — 5 drops

Dream Life
Geranium — 3 drops
Lemon — 2 drops
Neroli — 3 drops
Rosemary — 3 drops
Sandalwood — 3 drops

Meditation #2
Geranium — 2 drops
Juniper — 3 drops
Lavender — 3 drops
Lemon — 8 drops

Practice is already
enlightenment.

∽ Zen Master Dogen

In the sacred bedroom, choose your aromas carefully and with intent, being cautious not to overdo it. Select a scent to your liking for meditation and one for lovemaking. Rotate your chosen scents and blends or change them on a monthly basis if you wish. Using fewer is preferred because then you can use them to help ritualize specific bedroom activities. (We will look at rituals and ceremonies in chapter 5.) Make your fragrances a part of your experience of the sacred by keeping your oils with your altar supplies.

If you prefer not to invest in essential oils, you can explore the sense of smell by burning incense. Incense can be purchased in stores in the form of cones, coils, powders, or sticks. For example, light incense on your altar for use during meditation. The aroma will last for hours and help you associate the scent with the peaceful space you achieve during meditation. Once you select a fragrance for meditation, reserve it for meditation only, and avoid using it anywhere else in the house. In this way the scent will have only one association. It is best not to use essential oils and incense together, because too many strong scents may not produce a pleasing effect.

With the importance of the bedroom in our lives so clearly established, the scriptural sources explored, and the space arranged for maximum energy and best use for sacred activities, let's begin using the room for self-healing, worship, meditation, and exploring the world of dreams.

A Recipe for a Good Night's Sleep

Use an aromatherapy recipe for a good night's sleep. Especially helpful is chamomile, either German or Roman. Before bed, sip a cup of chamomile tea. Place a drop or two of chamomile essential oil in your burner or diffuser. Lavender is also a good fragrance for relaxation.

Again and again look within thine own mind.

∽ Padma-Sambhava

4

Your Inner Space

The human heart has hidden treasures,
In secret kept, in silence sealed.

— Charlotte Brontë, *Evening Solace*

The full flower of the sacred bedroom blooms in its role as a communication center to the Divine. With the arts of prayer, meditation, and dream guidance, the sacred holds us in its arms until morning. These tools can help you calm your mind and cultivate a temple consciousness whenever you enter your nighttime workshop.

PRAYER'S PRIVATE ROLE

The sacred bedroom holds the riches of a personal sanctuary and the unlimited potential of a new spiritual resource in your home. It is a sacred space that you have recovered from the gray landscape of everyday life, and it is all your own. The bedroom is more personal and intimate than a conventional place of worship. It is your private setting in which to rediscover your place in the universe as an inseparable companion of Spirit.

The potential for spiritual renewal and strength is unleashed in an enlightened mind and heart. Your sacred bedroom is the perfect place to fulfill that potential, and the power of prayer rightfully belongs there. You can use the bedroom to speak to the Creator without the need for intercession by others. You can turn your beliefs into action and express your needs in a formalized way to the Highest Force of all.

In addition to praying for particular things, consider praying whenever you enter or leave the bedroom, when you begin your day, and before you turn in to sleep. You can also pray before and after making love. You may use prayers of your chosen religion, mantras, affirmations, or chants. Chant phrases or prayer syllables are used repetitively, and Eastern teachings tell us that the sound and repetition harmonizes with universal vibration, thereby aligning our energies with the universal.

Prayer is used to communicate with the Creator through the deliberate use of will, generally for the following reasons:

- *Petition:* To ask for things or situations for yourself and others.

- *Confession:* To unburden the heart of a troubling mistake and to seek forgiveness.

- *Thanksgiving:* Expressing gratitude for the blessings in life.

- *Adoration:* To express praise to the Creator and adore the beauty of Spirit.

Prayer is powerful, especially when expressed aloud, because the power of sound drives the message or request into the atmospheres of air and thought. People who pray have known for millennia that prayer works. It works for healing, intercession, protection, and deliverance. For those who require the confirmation of science, research begun in the late 1970s showed that seriously ill patients, all receiving the same level of medical care, recovered more quickly if people were praying for them. A Duke University study in 1998 verified this finding in an experiment in which heart surgery patients were prayed for by prayer groups around the world, representing Christian, Jewish, and Buddhist religions. Recovery for

> Whatever you ask in prayer, you will receive if you have faith.
>
> ∞ Jesus,
> Matthew 21:22

these patients was 50 to 100 percent higher than for those who received no prayer.

Each religious tradition holds sacred its prayers and rituals. Is one way right and another wrong? Not according to the world's scriptures. Religion scholar Huston Smith, Ph.D., wrote in his *The World's Religions,* "What a strange fellowship this is. The God-seekers of every clime, lifting their voices in the most diverse ways imaginable to the God of all men. How does it all sound to Him? Like bedlam? Or, in some mysterious way, does it blend into harmony?" Something mystical happens during prayer. It engages the heart and elevates the mind to an extraordinary state. It also frees our minds from troubling thoughts.

When you pray, use your bedroom fully. Pray in a side chair, on the floor before your altar, or on your bed. Use forms of prayer that have meaning for you, perhaps prayers from your childhood, or seek new prayers from other traditions to which you inwardly respond. You can also compose your own prayers from the heart or pray spontaneously, speaking into the ether whatever is on your mind. The key is sincerity — if a message is alive in your heart, it will be alive in your words. Your voice will blend into the planetary song projecting ever outward, and inward, to I AM.

If you share your bedroom with a partner, it will be important to discuss with him or her how prayer will be coordinated — if at all. You may pray together or individually at different times. In the sacred bedroom, some of the most deeply personal and spiritual experiences are those we share with another. Uniting our spiritual efforts with another person helps us gain insights, new learning, and dissolve the self-centered ego that is at the root of many of our problems.

The bedroom is the place where the curtains are drawn and sheaths slide to the floor. It is where we stand naked, physically, mentally, emotionally, before God — and it's all right to be who we are. The bedroom is the crucible, the temple, where genuine expressions of love, emotion, hope, heartbreak, triumph, contentment, bring to the surface that part of you, the soul, that grows in spurts during peak experiences of intimacy: these are rare outside of the bedroom, and in the chamber of rest we can use these experiences to rediscover the authentic self of our childhood.

> It is vain for you to rise up early, to sit up late, to eat the bread of sorrows; for so he giveth his beloved sleep.
>
> ⮜ Psalm 127:2

The bedroom is where we are closest to God, because it is closest to the soul, that conscious knowledge that I am the best I there is, with no masks or costumes on the body or the mind. It is where the phrase "Oh God!" has never been more sincere, when prayer is fueled by a fiery heart and a tearful eye.

Even when negative circumstances are great and unavoidable in your life, you can secure a good portion of every day being free of those circumstances by keeping a certain space within you reserved for peace and quiet. The way to create that space within is through the practice of meditation.

THE KNEE OF LISTENING

The importance of attitude cannot be stressed enough as we seek solace and healing in the sacred bedroom. In terms of spiritual awareness, we can live happier lives in general if we learn to control and focus the mind. This is the great gift of meditation: the art of listening that is possible when the ego bends its knee in humility. We can employ the idea of "inner feng shui" to help us open up to the idea of controlling our thoughts and feelings.

Traditional feng shui seeks to cure poor energy flow in physical spaces, for example, curing a desk corner with a plant, avoiding a mirror facing the bed, or angling the bed so it does not point toward the door. However, there is a more holistic approach to feng shui that comes out of the Black Hat sect of Tibetan Tantric Buddhism — the very sect of the fourteen-year-old Karmapa Lama who escaped to India from Tibet in January 2000. The Black Hat sect approach, taught by Professor Thomas Lin Yun of the Lin Yun Temple, Berkeley, California, adds a personal spiritual perspective as we turn the bedroom into a sacred space.

Professor Lin Yun teaches a holistic approach to solving the problems of life. Instead of curing only the physical spaces and objects of a room, the practitioners of Black Hat Buddhist feng shui maintain that problems must also be solved by curing ourselves — correcting our personal *ch'i* through the use of meditation. In other words, yes, we create problems for ourselves that are beyond the reach of feng shui, but by clearing blocks and

> The fruit and the purpose of prayer is to be one with and like God in all things.
>
> ☙ Julian of Norwich

limitations within ourselves, we can work hand in hand with feng shui and make better use of *ch'i.*

Meditation is a practice that helps us discipline the mind, work around our emotions, be free from the influence of existential desires, and guard against negative thinking. It also helps us free ourselves from the ravages of stress, because when we meditate regularly, we are able to visit that peaceful childhood space within us that does not know the meaning of fear or doubt. Meditation works like a leash on the mind, which has been likened to a drunken monkey or an untrained puppy.

The art of focusing the mind is one of our greatest tools, because with it we can live life more efficiently and make fewer mistakes.

In *Meditation: An Eight-Point Program for Translating Spiritual Ideas into Everyday Life,* master teacher Eknath Easwaran, founder of the Blue Mountain Meditation Center, Tomales, California, defines meditation as "a systematic technique for taking hold and concentrating to the utmost degree our latent mental power. It consists in training the mind, especially attention and the will, so that we can set forth from the surface level of consciousness and journey into the very depth." He refers to deep meditation as a "return from exile," where we can regain our "vast inner treasure."

Meditation is our means of being in control of our thoughts and feelings, rather than being ruled by them. It is the great engine of refreshment and guidance that can be used in the unique solitary space of the sacred bedroom. Meditation can help us heal and unify the authentic self and allow it — rather than the selfish ego — its rightful place as ruler of the heart. Simple techniques include meditation while getting ready in the morning, starting or ending the day, and going deeper into one's spiritual life by spending time in an oasis apart from our desires and fears.

Meditation practices come out of nearly every spiritual tradition, each of which offers particular benefits. The goal is neither to "go blank" nor to simply apply concentration to a problem, such as when you are working out a relationship or planning a job change. The idea is to focus attention cleanly, clearly, on either some spiritual objective or simply the emptiness of silence. With

It is meditation that leads us in spirit into the hallowed solitudes wherein we find God alone — in peace, in calm, in silence, in recollection.

⁓ J. Crasset,
A Key to Meditation

When I'm operating at my best, my work is my prayer. It comes out of the same place that prayer comes out of — the center, the heart.

∽ Matthew Fox,
Creation Spirituality

practice, you are no longer distracted by the outside world, your senses, or the wanderings of your mind.

There are many techniques. You can investigate meditation practices from various traditions — Buddhist, yogic, even Christian — but to get started, you may care to try the simple steps below, steps that incorporate many of the main points shared by most of the systems. This meditation practice is nondenominational — it has to do with the mind and self-discipline. You can add to the practice as much as you wish and custom fit it to your needs. Use this simple method for all the meditation exercises in this book.

Achieving a meditative state requires four basic components:

1. **Comfort:** Whenever you can, meditate in front of your altar. You may sit upright in a comfortable chair or be seated on the floor in the cross-legged lotus position or with your legs folded beneath you. You may employ a cushion, such as a *zafu,* or meditation bench (see the "Resource Directory" at the end of the book). When you meditate, you want to be free from discomfort, but not so comfortable that you fall asleep. Meditate in the same place whenever possible. It is said that when engaging the sacred during meditation, the spiritual energy of your experiences remains in the place and builds as time goes on. The beauty of the energy you build in your sacred bedroom will greet and cheer you every time you enter there.

2. **Awareness of the breath:** Once you are comfortable, close your eyes and inhale deeply through your nose. Then exhale slowly through the mouth. Think about the breath at first, the feeling, the sound. Remember that, along with air, you are also breathing *ch'i,* called *prana* in Sanskrit. When you inhale, remember Huston Smith's words: "The brain breathes mind as the lungs breathe air." Imagine *ch'i* filling your lungs, radiating throughout your body to your head, arms and legs, fingertips and toes. When you exhale, visualize your worries, problems, and even illness leaving

your body like smoke. You can work your way out of any negative feeling by slowing, deepening, and moderating the rhythm of your breathing. Breathe in this manner for nine cycles to attain a state of physical peace and quiet.

3. **Enjoyment of the silence:** Success at achieving stillness will come gradually. When thoughts intrude, let them pass the way clouds pass across the sky while you are lying in the sun. Do the same with distractions of the senses: While we want to attune the senses in our enjoyment of the sacred bedroom, during meditation we treat sensory input the same way as passing thoughts. If you hear something during meditation, let it pass. Be the observer and don't allow thoughts to engage you or carry you away with them; when they threaten to do so, return to the peaceful place within. With practice, the clear spaces *between thoughts* will widen. Work toward sustaining this peaceful space for two to three minutes at a time.

4. **Engagement of the mind with a meditative focus:** Some people use meditation for clearing the mind and waiting to see what comes in. I call this passive meditation, preferring instead active meditation, in which you engage the peaceful mind with some focus pertaining to your spiritual ideal. Choose a passage from the Bible, for example, the Bhagavad Gita, or the teachings of Buddha. Focus on a quotation for a full five minutes, delving deeper and deeper into its obvious and hidden meanings. Consider meditating on the image of God within you. On the spiritual foundation of your sexual and sensual feelings. On your masculine and feminine nature. You can write the harvest of your meditations into a journal and collect them, or simply enjoy the insights that emerge.

> When we think our prayers have not been answered, we should not become saddened over it. I am certain that God is telling us that we must wait for a better time, more grace, or that a better gift will be given us.
>
> ᜫ Julian of Norwich

You can enhance your meditation experience by incorporating prayer before and after each session. I like to use the prayer of Francis of Assisi, saying the first half at the beginning of meditation and the second half on closing:

Lord, make me an instrument of thy peace.

Where there is hatred, let me sow love;
Where there is injury, pardon;
Where there is doubt, faith;
Where there is despair, hope;
Where there is darkness, light;
Where there is sadness, joy.

O Divine Master, grant that I may not so much seek
To be consoled as to console;
To be understood as to understand;
To be loved as to love;
For it is in giving that we receive;
It is in pardoning that we are pardoned;
It is in dying that we are born to eternal life.

> The knowledge that comes through dreaming is absolute because it comes from a level of symbolic association that is deeper than consciousness.
>
> ∾ Robin Ridington, anthropologist

The key to success in meditation is regular practice, because even if you think you are not making progress, you really are — you will "awaken" to this success eventually, realizing that you really are finding a peaceful place within you. Practice is vital, even taking five minutes in the morning and evening. Think of meditation as your special opportunity to bask in the peaceful place in your heart — the place that is close to the center of you, close to the I AM within you. In meditation, with spiritual motivation you can become one with the I AM; the divine inner identity of God-Is-Love within you. Let your bedroom temple be the haven where you regularly contact the silent beauty that lives in your heart.

Essential Oils for Meditation

Lavender	Bergamot
Frankincense	Jasmine
Rose otto	Cypress
Sandalwood	Geranium
Cedarwood	Ylang Ylang

THE GIFT OF SLEEP

When you lay your head down at night, you are never truly alone, because you are sleeping with 250 million people! This simple calculation, dividing the world's 6 billion people by the twenty-four time zones, reveals the fact that around the same time you are turning in beneath your matching sheets, someone in the rain forest has just lain down on a palette of leaves, and an Inuit has just climbed with his whole community onto their skin-covered shelf on the ice. So it goes as the day closes its eye in the endless roll of night and day around the earth.

All the creatures of the world sleep: bats upside down, sharks as they swim, and foxes in burrows. Fully one-third of our lives is spent in bed, whether on leaves, ice, a tatami, factory-sewn mattresses, in sleeping bags, racks, bunks, singles, doubles, queens, or kings. Sleep is one sacred bedroom activity that is vital to our health.

We all sleep, but when we wake up in the morning, we have different stories to tell. One wakes up grouchy, having "gotten up on the wrong side of the bed," while another awakens refreshed and alert, greeting the morning with a grateful grin and shake of the hair. One can roll out of bed exhausted, as though he or she labored, fought, or ran all night. Still another is red eyed, waking in disarray, having tossed and turned and checked the clock throughout the night.

Sleep is not only important for our rest, but essential to our spiritual, mental, emotional, and physical health. Not just any kind of sleep will do, for there is good sleep and bad sleep, and each has its effects on the quality of our lives, personalities, and relationships.

What we call sleep is actually a vivid nightlife filled with events and a set of patterns that convey us through the night. Once we fall asleep, we sleep deeply without dreams for about ninety minutes. We then have three to four dreaming periods until we awaken in the morning. Just before going to sleep and just after waking up, we pass into a state of consciousness that is neither sleep nor truly wakefulness; the former is called hypnogogic sleep and the latter hypnopompic sleep. In these states we can feel

> Meditation is like a needle after which comes a thread of gold, composed of affections, prayers, and resolutions.
>
> ✍ St. Alphonsus

inspired, like we're floating, receive ideas or guidance from within. Writers, artists, scientists, and inventors throughout the ages have attested to the creative ideas they have received during these transitions to and from sleep. (See "The Muse of Sleep" chart below.)

Jean Cocteau's play
Knights of the Round Table
was inspired by a dream

The Muse of Sleep

Many authors attribute the creation of characters, chapters, and entire works to their dreams. Such authors and examples include

- Robert Louis Stevenson, *The Strange Case of Dr. Jekyll and Mr. Hyde*
- William Burroughs
- Robert Penn Warren
- Jack Kerouac, whose characters appeared in his dreams
- Graham Greene, *It's a Battlefield* and *Honorary Consul*
- Charlotte Brontë, who used dreams as a tool to break writer's block
- John Masefield, his poem "The Woman Speaks"
- Voltaire, his canto "La Henriade" and other works
- Johann W. von Goethe

Psychologists have begun mapping the journey we take at night and have a way of measuring the rising and falling of consciousness during sleep. To sleep well, you should fall asleep naturally, without the use of drugs. You should wake up rarely during the night and awaken naturally in the morning, refreshed and alert, but never groggy or anxious. A good sleep sustains you throughout the day with plenty of energy, and, unless your lunch contains a lot of sugar or alcohol, you should not find yourself dozing in midday.

We each have different needs, and not everyone requires eight hours of sleep. For example, I need seven, whereas my wife requires a full eight. Try turning in earlier or setting your alarm later, if schedules permit: You may need more sleep than you think you do.

As we saw in the previous section, stress is the great enemy of our health, relationships, efficiency, and happiness. Stress and poor sleep work hand in hand to deteriorate our health: When we are stressed, we do not sleep well; when we do not sleep well, it makes us more prone to stress.

The secret to getting a good night's sleep is taking practical steps to eliminate conditions that rob you of your sleep. In order of importance, they are

Effects of stress: Use the steps in the first section of chapter 3 to control or eliminate the influence of stress on your sleep.

Worry: While stress can set you up for a fitful sleep, worry can keep your eyes open all night. Use the techniques described in chapter 3 for conquering stress. In addition, work with your Spiritual Ideals Statement, change your attitude, meditate often, and leave worries outside the bedroom on a piece of paper. Approach sleep with a slogan: "Thank God for sleep! My personal license to suspend my worries until morning!"

Discomfort: In chapter 2, we discussed beds, furnishings, and the design of your room. Look carefully at the temperature and humidity of your room, conditions of dust, and any allergenic substances. Look at your spread, blankets, sheets, what they are made of, and how they feel against your skin.

Food: Eating too close to bedtime forces the system to be "active" in the process of digestion. A system that is digesting is not resting. Avoid stimulants such as caffeine, sugar, and spicy foods.

Alcohol and other drugs: "Sleeping it off" doesn't mean quality sleep, as alcohol can stimulate nightmares. When you awaken hung over, you have not had a quality sleep. Even though you were "out like a light," you were out on the inside, too.

Babies, children: Every parent is familiar with this one, and there is little that one can do, especially in the case of an infant, whose needs take precedence over your good night's sleep. The best way to prepare yourself to get both jobs done is to give yourself a pre-sleep suggestion — a self-hypnosis technique — telling yourself that the child you love is part of your night life for those few years of infancy. Awaken to the child's call gratefully, take in a deep breath, and say to your baby: "I choose to stay relaxed while I take care of you, and then slip back into deep sleep, so I can be refreshed to take care of you tomorrow." Older children should be taught not to make unnecessary noise at night.

Bedtime Story

During the Renaissance, women in Europe lay for the first time on black satin sheets to show off their porcelain skin to best effect. Beds, often as large as eight feet by seven feet, were carved and hung with beautiful fabrics. Different woods, inlaid stones, shining metals, abundant quilting, and smooth hangings of silk and velvet came into use, which was the first time since ancient civilizations that the bedroom showed signs of becoming a place of honor and beauty.

෴

A description of the Holocaust was published in 1881 by Rabbi Hile Wechsler, who dreamed it in astonishing detail.

Partners: Partners have different habits, demands, and needs and can sometimes be disruptive to our sleep. Different retiring or rising times, for example, can disturb one or the other partner. There can also be snoring, nocturnal trips to the bathroom, teeth grinding (the result of the partner's stress), talking or walking in their sleep, or a sudden, urgent request for sex (a majority of men and women often exhibit the physical signs of sexual excitement during REM sleep). Some interruptions are more desirable than others, but they can all disturb our sleep.

Noise: The dreaming mind takes normal external stimuli and presents them in the language of dreams: a speeding motorcycle passing your window can turn into a bright, angry bird. If you live on a noisy street, try to seal or insulate your windows. You can also purchase a sleep machine, which can provide white noise, rolling surf, or rain sounds. A tabletop water fountain can also be used to drown out unwanted noise.

Pets: I have a small, striped cat named Douglas Fur. He occasionally wakes my wife and me between three and four o'clock in the morning. He does this with his paws, gently putting them on a cheek, nose, or forehead. If we turn over, he touches the nape of the neck. The solution to this sort of interruption is to keep the door closed. We have elected not to do this and simply take our lumps. I have, however, trained Douglas to expect better results by waking my wife more often than me.

Nightmares: We have all been awakened by nightmares. They can simply be the result of the waking mind's misinterpretation of the normal before it is fully awake, or a result of the suppression of fear and doubts, which we are either unaware of or unwilling to deal with during our waking lives. (Recurring nightmares or unusual sleep disturbances warrant professional help.)

Naturally, you will never get to sleep if you try to think of all these things as you are snapping off the light. Just being aware of them from day to day can help you regard your bedroom as your personal haven of peace and regeneration, nurturing, and safety. Once there, realize that this utmost important third of your life is vital for your health and happiness.

We have all had the experience of lying awake for hours, tossing and turning, and trying everything from commanding ourselves to sleep to begging God to allow it to happen. Not even exhaustion and fatigue are enough to drive us to sleep, if our worries are chronic and the habit of stress has been learned by the body. Of course, sleep can neither be persuaded nor coerced. This is because sleep is a result: It is the condition that remains once the thoughtful mind finally "gives it up," gives up its preoccupations, analysis, wishes, demands, and even reveries. To go to sleep, all you need to do is stop being aware of yourself. Don't allow yourself to observe yourself anymore.

In *Restful Sleep*, Deepak Chopra, M.D., advises us to "just rest comfortably, not minding, and use this attitude as a way of placing yourself in nature's hands. Simply lie in bed with your eyes closed, not minding whether you're awake or asleep. The mere act of remaining motionless with your eyes closed, even if you're feeling anxious or restless, actually provides the body with significant benefits."

> Without knowledge
> there is no meditation,
> without meditation there
> is no knowledge.
> He who has knowledge
> and meditation is near
> to Nirvana.
>
> ∾ **The Dhammapada**

PERCHANCE TO DREAM

Sleep is just the beginning of our nighttime connection to the Divine. Just as 250 million people leave their waking consciousness of rational thought, they enter the nighttime consciousness of dreams, where surreal images and scenes are the norm. The mysterious night school of our inner learning takes place in a classroom with those 250 million people who are simultaneously engaged in dream life under the tutelage of the wisdom of the Higher Self — our soul's consciousness where true wisdom resides within us.

During the night, we have several periods of satisfying dreaming, which turns out to be even more important than sleep in keeping us rested and healthy. During the 1950s, Nathaniel Kleitman and his students at the University of Chicago discovered that people who are deprived of their dreams begin to act anxious, hostile, and resentful. They tend to use poor judgment, drink or smoke more, and lose their ability to think creatively. Those who are awakened during nondream periods show no effects. The point is that, unlike what was previously thought, we do not sleep in order to rest. We sleep in order to dream.

We can honor the bedroom's ability to heal; the sacred bedroom is the portal between two worlds, the waking world and the subconscious world of our dreams. Sleep is the reception room for our communion with the Divine, a chamber that houses the body when consciousness steps out of its protective clothes of responsibilities, ego, and control and slips into something more comfortable — the dream state, in which we are within touching distance of the sacred.

The sacred nature of dreams is supported by Robert L. Van de Castle, former director of the Sleep and Dream Laboratory at the University of Virginia and professor in the Department of Behavioral Medicine, in his book *Our Dreaming Mind.*

"Dreams have not only led to scientific and artistic developments," he writes, "but have also served as channels for spiritual inspiration. Some form of dream imagery is embedded in the beginnings of most of the world's major religions." Dreams are honored in most of the major religions as links to the mind of the Creator.

The Bible gives us, "For God speaks in one way, and in two, though man does not perceive it. In a dream, in a vision of the night, when deep sleep falls upon men, while they slumber on their beds, then he opens the ears of men. . . . " (Job 33:14–16) We also find the well-known quote from Joel 2:28: "And it shall come to pass afterward, that I will pour out my spirit on all flesh; your sons and your daughters shall prophesy, your old men shall dream dreams, and your young men shall see visions."

Other biblical dreams are well known, from Jacob's dream of angels ascending and descending the ladder to the dream in which God told him he would be given the land upon which he slept. (Genesis 28:12–17) Many of the Roman Catholic saints had the "gift" of dreams, for example, Fr. Giovanni Bosco, who received guidance from dreams all his life, and Francis of Assisi, who was guided in his ministry through dreams, seven of which were recorded.

That happiness which belongs to a mind which by deep meditation has been washed clear of all impurity and has entered within the Self, cannot be described by words; it can be felt by the inward power only.

ᔆ The Upanishads

Van de Castle's study of dreams over many years has led him to conclude in *Our Dreaming Mind,* "Aside from their role in the development of specific religions, dreams have suggested answers to many pervasive and eternal questions: Who are we? Where did we come from? Why are we here? Of what are we made? Where are we going? What is death? Is there an existence after death? If there is an existence, of what does it consist? People of all times have pondered these tenacious and troubling questions. What is seldom recognized is that dreams have helped to provide some answers."

Dreams are the nightly letters we write to ourselves in an intimate language of symbols, skits, and scenarios unrestricted by the harnesses of time and place. Dreams are instructive lessons designed by the Higher Self using the secret language and symbols of our own thoughts, feelings, and memories. Your dreams are all about *you*: what is going on in your personality, relationships, and life generally, what occurred the day of the dream, and internal conflicts that have plagued you for years.

In our dreams we can find wisdom's counsel. They are the storybooks whose morals can teach us, if we know how to read the signs and understand the messages that we are showing to ourselves. The messages come to us dressed up as our familiar people, places, and objects. Most modern dream researchers agree that dreams have specific purposes in our lives. All we have to do is choose to learn from them. Dreams can

- Give us insights into activities and relationships

- Indicate a need for change in attitude or habits

- Encourage us to take new directions in life

- Reveal our ignored talents or abilities

- Help us identify negative behavior

- Help us to help others

In the day-to-day world, we unknowingly navigate in an ocean of moods, issues, frustrations, sorrows, and joys that paint our dreams with a palette of archetypes that spill back and forth between the ego and the mirror of the soul. Even though we do

> Let us learn to dream, gentlemen, and then we may perhaps find the truth.
>
> ∽ Friedrich A. von Kekule, nineteenth-century chemist

not always remember our dreams, researchers hold that each one of us dreams three or four times every night.

Dreams come in many forms and for many purposes. Most are either literal (a review of the activities of the day), wish fulfillment, self-compensating, or symbolic of real-life situations. Scott Cunningham, in *Sacred Sleep: Dreams and the Divine*, maintains that one can engage in "sacred sleep" by preparing and asking for a dream for the purpose of eliciting divine guidance. Dreams, he maintains, are a means of contacting the Divine and receiving an answer that you can remember and record in the morning.

We can use dreams as tools for better understanding ourselves and guiding our lives using the following simple technique for recording and interpreting them.

UNDERSTANDING YOUR DREAMS

Dreams are an ordered kaleidoscope of the contents of your psyche. Frustration with a relationship becomes two animals that cannot understand one another; an elderly person dying represents your old self after a change in your life; fears stand naked in front of a classroom or careen down a hill out of control; an attic becomes a symbol for your Higher Self.

A growing number of psychologists suggest that we can work with the symbols of our dreams to gain insights into our personalities, receive guidance for making decisions, and even commune with the sacred. If you are interested in exploring these intimate messages you receive in the bedroom, I suggest you experiment with a simple plan.

Select a night that's free from the influences of sugar, alcohol, and other artificial stimulants (including TV). Choose a night when you have had time to relax at least an hour before bed and when the next morning will give you time to write down your dream. Remembering, recording, and working with dreams become easy the more you do them, but this is a good way to begin. Remember that if you have not been getting enough sleep or are overtired, dream recall will come less easily.

Anyone can begin working with dreams by being organized

A dream which is not understood is like a letter which is not opened.

෨ The Talmud

and by following a few simple steps. There are variations on these steps, depending on who you read. However, the following steps have worked well for me over the years.

The very act of preparing for a dream primes your subconscious mind to produce one that you will remember in the morning. You can formalize this act by beginning with a "dream petition" that you write on a piece of paper and place under your pillow before going to sleep. Write down the purpose of the petition and the result you expect to receive: "I petition my Higher Self to give me a dream this night to show me how to get along better with my partner. Show me how I can remedy the situation."

WORKING WITH YOUR DREAMS

Step 1: Record the dream. Place a notebook and pen for recording your dreams by your bedside. Details of dreams can vanish quickly after waking, so when you wake from a dream, you want to record the details as soon as possible. Keep a flashlight nearby as well, so if you wake from a dream during the night, you can record it without disturbing your partner. Keeping a dream notebook will help you be able to come back later and look at the symbology as well as patterns over the long run. Record the events of your dream in order and with as much detail as you can remember. A tape recorder can also be used if you wish to describe the dream verbally.

It often happens that once you begin writing down your dreams you will remember them more often, and it will become easier to record them. With some practice, you will be able to understand your dreams without even having to write them down.

Step 2: Make a theme statement. After you have written down the dream, create a "theme statement," a single sentence, that captures what happened. In this theme statement, intentionally avoid referring to details, symbols, or the personalities involved. Instead, use the words "someone," "something," and "somewhere." As an example, I use a recent dream of my own.

I'm driving a miniature Model T around the grounds of my place of work, trying to get up the hill to my office. I

> In dreams we see ourselves naked and acting out our real characters, even more clearly than we see others awake.
>
> ∽ Henry David Thoreau

Dreams are the true
Interpreters of our
Inclinations; but there is
Art required to sort and
understand them.

∽ Montaigne, *Essays*

cannot find the familiar road. Then I see an Asian master, leading a group in meditation. He smiles at me, and I understand that I can choose to follow him anytime I wish or continue to struggle trying to find the road to my office. I hesitate, and at that instant, a man with a gun appears and threatens to shoot me.

I summarized the theme by writing: "Someone can't get some-where, then someone else invites him to follow the spiritual path." I filled in the details later, but setting the theme helped me remember that all the people in the dream are parts of myself. In this way, when I try to learn what the dream is saying, I'll be concentrating on the parts rather than giving importance to other "people." When you are writing down the theme, be creative, playful, even humorous. If you are like me, then you may have long "produc-tion number" dreams with two and three parts. If this is the case, each part can have its own theme.

Step 3: Describe feelings. After you have written down the theme, write down what you felt during the dream and then how you felt upon waking. In the dream above, I remembered feeling frustrated and foolish. As I wrote out my theme and emotional responses, I was feeling "embarrassed." These sorts of feelings are your first indications of what a dream means. Had I been angry in the dream or sobbing, the meaning would be colored differently. I later reasoned that I was feeling foolish about neglecting my spir-itual life. Remember that dreams, and all their symbols, are about you and various aspects of your personality.

Step 4: Compare. Now, compare the theme to what's going on in your life. This could be a particular problem that has been bothering you, a sequence of activities, a long-standing problem with which you are struggling. You wrote the theme statement simply so you are not working too intimately with the issues of your waking consciousness too soon in the process. The dream above took place during a time in my life when I was obsessed with my job and procrastinating about my spiritual growth. During the comparison step, I linked the "someone" who can't get to work to my frustration. In this step, write down any insights that come to you. As you think about the dream, your subconscious can inspire you with insights about its meaning. Again, don't begin interpreting just yet. Just write down the similarities between themes in your life and the theme of the dream.

Step 5: Examine symbols. Now you can look at the details of the dream. First, note the symbols that provoked you or that stood out prominently in the dream, and what those symbols have generally meant to you in your life. While there are some symbol archetypes that seem universal (see "Some Universal Dream Symbols" on page 98), dream symbols are still very personal, and their meanings can change from one person to another, or even at different times in your life. For example, to one person, finding a wallet symbolizes discovering some unknown or undeveloped talent. To another, it symbolizes an abusive father or a challenge about honesty, guilt about a theft of money, or acclaim. In my dream example, the Model T, as a primitive means of transportation, symbolizes childishness; the Asian master, who reminds me of Buddha or Lao-tzu, represents my Higher Self revealing a lesson to me.

Step 6: Apply. The purpose of looking for meaning in your dreams is lost if you don't find ways to use the insights they offer you. My dream above revealed to me that I was being foolish in my attitude toward my job — the miniature Model T indicated that I was being childish, underusing my capacity, and using my job as an excuse not to pursue my spiritual life. My interpretation led me to conclude that it was only my attitude that was holding me back spiritually. The man with the gun was simply a mandate I was giving myself to make a choice. If I didn't soon choose, I would be killing myself with responsibilities and ensuring that I might soon be spiritually "dead," unable to move, either in my career or in my spiritual life.

By using this technique regularly, understanding your dreams will come more easily over time. Eventually, you may not even have to record your dreams — the meanings will become clear to you as you review their contents. In the beginning, however, you can facilitate remembering and recording your dreams if you "program" yourself the night before with a request to your subconscious. I

Bedtime Story

In the nineteenth century a maharajah ordered a silver bed from Paris with each of its four posts in the form of a life-size nude woman. The women had real hair and blue enamel eyes, and carried fans that moved when the maharajah lay down. His weight activated a music box that played "God Save the Queen."

❧

suggest using the following prayer or affirmation, or one that is to your liking:

> I request a dream this night to instruct me on [insert problem or issue]. I will wake up with a full memory of the dream and my feelings, which will remain fresh until I am finished writing them down. I will be inspired to understand the dream and its instructive message to me.

As you record your dreams over time, you can spot repeating patterns among the themes. Largely, these will indicate a persistent problem or some blindness that you continue to carry with you. When this is the case, you can "incubate" a dream with the affirmation above to help you understand this long-standing issue. Another tip for dream interpretation is to awaken gently from the dream state, rather than be wrenched awake by a loud alarm clock or clock radio.

Dream researchers agree that the symbols in individual dreams are keyed to that individual's life experiences and memories. However, there are some archetypal master symbols that seem to have universal functions among dreamers in the same culture. Some of these are described below, although you may wish to consult a dream dictionary or one of several good books on dream interpretation to find the style you like best. With each of these symbols, be sure to reflect on what personal meaning they had for you in the past as you seek meanings for your dreams. For example, note any unusual features that add extremes (a *giant* carrot vs. a *green* carrot) or distortions (a *bumpy* mirror vs. a *cloudy* mirror) to the symbols, and let the meanings reveal themselves to you.

SOME UNIVERSAL DREAM SYMBOLS

Animals: What kind of animal is it? How does the animal look and act? Animals are often symbols for some negative aspect of yourself. They represent your lower nature; for example, your appetites, how you go about attaining your desires, the way you treat others, or your selfish habits. A rat could represent guilt; a squirrel, disorganization; a butterfly, superficiality in relationships.

One hour's sleep before midnight is worth two hours after.

      A proverb

Automobiles: An automobile can represent your physical vehicle in life (your body) or your personal resources. Unwanted passengers can represent habits or relationships that you are taking with you that you don't like. A car without brakes can indicate a need for restraint in some aspect of your life. The car represents the way you move forward in your life, how you are getting to your goals.

Being chased: In our dreams, we are chased by animals, people, trees, storms, and even unspecified, scary forces. We try desperately to escape the danger, and often wake up sweating and out of breath. This is the classic clue that there is some part of yourself, your work, your personality, or your social life that you are trying to escape. Sometimes we are being chased by fear itself!

Setting: Locations can show you the department of your life that needs attention. The kitchen may indicate eating habits; the office, your job or work situation or attitude toward them. A police station could mean that some aspect of your life needs "policing," while a hospital may indicate that your health needs attention. A road indicates your path in life.

Clothing: Clothes symbolize your various roles in life and also your attitude. Clothes that don't fit right could indicate a role in which you don't feel comfortable or an attitude you have adopted that just isn't "you." Clothing symbolizes the façade you show the world and also the emotional shell you use to protect yourself from it.

Death: A death in a dream does not indicate that someone is going to die, but rather that some part of you has undergone a change — that some old habit or aspect of your psyche is no longer alive in you. A dream death is thought to be a positive sign that you are changing, but it can also mean that you engage in self-destructive behavior. We can dream of death after we have overcome a nasty part of our personality and grown, or, if we've chosen the wrong path, we may be leaving behind an aspect of our personality that was good.

Falling: Most people dream of falling, which usually indicates a warning or feeling of failure, loss of status or reputation, or of being criticized. It can also mean feeling like you have no control,

> When you pray, go into your room and shut the door and pray to your Father who is in secret; and your Father who sees in secret will reward you.
>
> ∽ Jesus,
> Matthew 6:5–6

are losing your grasp, or are helpless in a situation or in life in general. The meaning changes if, instead of falling in terror, you are enjoying the fall, feeling free from the need to be in control of some situation.

Flying: Many of us remember the exhilaration of flying through the air in a dream. This is the classic symbol of feeling free of some burden, reminding you in your waking life to adopt a more grateful attitude. Trying to fly unsuccessfully can indicate something you are trying to "get off the ground," perhaps a relationship or a project. The setting, circumstances, and your own associations with these symbols will help you understand the specific message you need to hear.

Money: We have all dreamt of finding or losing money, but this rarely indicates the gain or loss of a fortune. Loss of money indicates a loss of self-worth or engaging in some wasteful activity, whereas finding money can mean discovering some new advantage, talent, or value in oneself, a relationship, or situation.

Having sex: Most people have had the experience of having sex in dreams, ranging from fulfilling true love with some ideal romantic partner to some sordid or absurd situation. We can be filled with longing and regret afterward, or even with embarrassment. Before interpreting, describe the partner, his or her attitude, the tone of the dream encounter, and how you felt in the dream. Remember, too, that a love partner can represent an aspect of yourself, symbolize the particulars of a relationship with a person or your attitude toward love itself.

People: The people in our dreams are aspects of our personalities. In each dream, there is a "you" observer and the other people you come in contact with. These others are the traits of your psyche that you either need to develop or get rid of. They may be the voice of your Higher Self, as the Asian master in my dream of the Model T, although your Higher Self can speak to you in many other guises. Again, use "someone" did "something" "somewhere." Then ask, "What am I trying to tell myself in that role?"

Being naked in public: Usually when we dream of being naked, we do not realize that we can find clothing or run away; we feel stuck in front of everyone. We are hotly embarrassed or

Even sleep has its purpose. The man who wishes to progress in his service always forward, from holiness to holiness, from world to world, must first put aside his life-work in order to receive a new spirit, whereby a new revelation may come upon him. And therein lies the secret of sleep. Yea, even sleep has its service.

≈ Louis I. Newman,
The Hasidic Anthology

ashamed in the dream, and it reveals a fear of being vulnerable, of a secret being revealed — a secret such as fears of inadequacy. Feeling comfortable naked in a dream can indicate comfort with one's body or sexuality. Having acted in the theater in my twenties, when I have these dreams I am not only naked — I can't remember my lines!

Inability to call out: This usually follows on the heels of a dream situation in which you are trapped or in danger. You hit the panic button and try to scream, but cannot. This is a classic dream message that there is something in your life or emotions with which you need help. This sometimes manifests as a listener who will not hear you or cannot understand you.

Water: Dreams use water in so many ways, there is no particular interpretation. The meaning for your dream could change depending on whether you are floating or sinking, being overwhelmed by a tidal wave or simply swimming in the sunrise. The literal often works in dream interpretation: an ocean of emotion, the stream of events, reality splashing you in the face. Again, look at what the particular symbol means to you in your memories, and that will help you understand its significance.

Dr. Van de Castle summarized the value of dreams best when he wrote, "Dreams can serve to dispel the lonely illusion of separateness we maintain during waking hours and reveal the many levels of interconnectedness which exist between us. These benefits can be reaped by starting to share our dreams with each other and learning to develop a greater appreciation of the power of our dreaming mind."

It may surprise you to think that the world of our dreams is closely related to romance, another aspect of our bedroom, that private place where we cherish our solitude, or imagine or entertain lovers. Next we will look at romance in a way that you may never have thought of before, and at ways in which we can bring our sacred bedrooms alive with ritual and ceremony.

Prayer ones the soul to God.

∽ Julian of Norwich

5

Romance and Rituals

Did my heart love till now? Forswear it, sight!
For I ne'er saw true beauty till this night.

— Shakespeare, *Romeo and Juliet*

For an individual, the sacred bedroom can become a personal sanctuary for communing with the Divine. However, the addition of a partner creates new opportunities as well as challenges. The bedroom is a couple's workshop in relationships, with the potential to become a temple of romance. It is a private haven for discovering your capacity for true love.

IN LOVE WITH ROMANCE

The bedroom is the playhouse of romance. Whether you and your partner are on fire with love or long-time marrieds whose youthful flames have tempered over time, you can deepen your relationship in a bedroom that is alive in the sacred. With spiritual understanding, you can discover that romance itself bears the imprint of the Divine. One way to find that divinity is to take a look at what we mean when we say we are "in love."

As there is wedlock
between a man and wife
so there is wedlock
between God
and the soul.

∽ Meister Eckhart

If only love were easy, our relationships would be trouble free. We would stay deliriously in love forever. When we fall in love, we melt into the belief that our loved one will fulfill all our hopes and dreams. We believe that person will please us, forgive our faults, and love us forever. Is it a coincidence that we attribute these same qualities to the Creator, with whom the soul, it is said, is perpetually in love?

When we're high on love, our spiritual lives tend to fade into the background of giddy happiness. This may be evidence enough that God-Is-Love surely blazes in the hearts of lovers. It's in the joy, a condition the Creator invented.

Our culture is in love with being in love. We long for arms to hold us, for the touch of warm skin and soft kisses. We desire devotion from that perfect other for whom we search and to whom we devote ourselves. When love is returned, confidence soars into the stratosphere. The whole world becomes magical. The air is alive. Strangers on the street seem to cheer for us. The park, the beach, the forest, or the library, wherever we play out our affections, belongs to us alone. When we are in love, our soul's delight crests above the surface. Being in love stimulates loving feelings from deep within us. Our need for love attracts us to ideas of romance, whatever we believe it to be.

Romance is the stepchild of the heroic love tales of ancient times that were published during the Middle Ages. These were the stories of idealized virtues, the knight in shining armor, abduction of the lady fair, and the arduous journey to rescue her. Romances depicted characters that showcased the constancy of the soul: pursuing the Holy Grail of spiritual truth; love's truth being freed, at last, from the castle keep of evil oppression.

Romance is crystallized in the symbol of two trees, growing forever from the graves of good Tristan and Iseult, their branches so closely intertwined that they can never be separated. Romance, as it used to be, still melts the sentimental heart and makes the eyes weep — romance novels account for more than half of all paperback books sold in the United States. Originally, romances were not about having sex. They were about the *getting there*.

In the twentieth century, many believe romance to be a myth, because those early virtuous ideals are laughed at. Mired in sexual fantasy, our modern notions of romance often leave love in the lurch. Books, magazines, films, and TV shows flood our consciousness with artificial charms. Genuine love is trampled by outer appearances — youthful good looks, sexiness, unconditional adoration, and snapping off the light with a snicker before the last commercial. Along the way, our attitudes about love and romance, as well as our self-worth, are shaped by these influences.

The ideals of medieval romance, however, reflected the template of Spirit echoed in the world's scriptures. Honor, fidelity, integrity, and devotion to love inspired the hearts of generations suppressed by religious orthodoxy. The truth is that being in love matches the pattern of God-Is-Love. Our male and female polarities magnify the divine image when hands join as one and some sweet gift is left on a pillow. The givingness spawned by romance meshes perfectly with the generosity of nature and Spirit alike.

The bedroom is romance's home base, so you can let your intimate, personal touches and gestures reflect a higher truth before your altar and in your bed. Whether or not you are in love at the moment, you can share the glorious feeling of being in love with the Creator, the source of all ecstasy, and being in love with your Divine Self. Find that beautiful, authentic self, forgive it, and honor it. Think of yourself as an imprint of the Creator. In that image, you will discover your integrity and your responsibility. You will reveal within yourself your own heroic character, a confident person of unwavering ideals that will be irresistible for attracting and keeping your "soul mate."

You can bring romance under the umbrella of the sacred by remembering that

- The lord or lady of the sacred bedroom deserves equal honor and respect.

- You don't have to be in love in order to be happy. You can learn to love yourself as the Creator loves you.

- The feeling of being in love is the innate love of the soul temporarily overwhelming the ego. Keep love alive when conditions begin to change.

All that we see or seem
Is but a dream
within a dream.

∞ Edgar Allan Poe,
"A Dream within
a Dream"

- You must nourish your spiritual life. Do as the Buddhists do, and acquire merit through right living. It will keep your heart open and help "being in love" last.

For romantics, flowers, candy, and candlelit dinners are still the tools of the trade. We use them to display the true affections that blaze on the altars of our hearts. We can deepen the value of romance and make love more durable if we open our hearts and add a sacred dimension.

Ten Ways to Open Your Heart

1. When some hurt occupies your thoughts, give service to all you meet.
2. Try to find the Divine in some aspect of everyone you know.
3. Remember to show your feelings and ask your partner for help in healing them.
4. Guard your speech so your words are never hurtful.
5. Practice silence when others need to express their views.
6. Show gratitude to people.
7. Spend a day discovering each ordinary thing as new and exciting.
8. Laugh often and make others laugh.
9. Cultivate the lightness and freedom of forgiveness.
10. Listen deeply until you understand another.

Here are some ideas on how to elevate romance into the spiritual, so that even when you are soaring in the stratosphere of being in love, your actions have a sacred intent that can withstand the test of time. These ideas can help you incorporate traditional romantic gestures into the hallowed setting of the sacred bedroom.

Candles: Romantics light candles for mood, whether for dinner or in the bedroom. Light those candles with the sacred intent that they symbolize the light of consciousness. Light two candles to represent the soul mates of you and your lover. Light one candle for the oneness that you make by being together. As you each light a candle, say the words: "I am honored to light your way" or "With this candle I honor the light of Spirit within you."

Small miracles
are all around us
We can find them
everywhere — in our
home, in our daily
activities, and, where they
are hardest to see,
in ourselves.

∽ Sue Bender

Communication: Observe how you communicate when you are in love. You are attentive and careful whenever you speak and you listen deeply. It makes your partner feel worthy and that what he or she has to say is important. Have reverence for the power of language to please or to hurt. If you do not understand each other, take the time to sort it out. Be open to change, as well as forgiveness. Try never to let the sun set on an argument.

Dancing: Dancing is symbolic of the primordial joining of forces that created the world. It is the union of energies, masculine and feminine, symbolizing the dance of the universe, and the joining and separating of polar opposites. When you dance, enjoy the fun. If you have not danced in ages, it is never too late. Enjoy the symbol you are making that harmonizes with the very core of the universe.

Flowers: Men typically send roses to their loved ones, but a potted flowering plant might better convey a deeper, long-lasting meaning. In the pot, a flower or houseplant symbolizes groundedness and longevity of your relationship into the future. Living plants add good feng shui to the bedroom. They give oxygen and remove carbon dioxide. After you have enjoyed your potted plant indoors, plant it in the yard. Consider a planting outside your bedroom window in full view. You can watch it grow as a symbol of your love and relationship and commemorate the day you planted it. Consider a camellia or rosebush.

Food: Food and romance are inseparable. Couples often go out to dinner or make dinner for each other. When you cook for your beloved, pray for healing, fidelity, and longevity. Do you wish to give candy? Invite your lover to make homemade truffles with you some Sunday afternoon: Infuse them with love. Eat them during a ceremony that you conduct in your sacred bedroom. Serve your lover breakfast in bed, and choose each item for its symbolic meaning.

Fragrances: In chapter 3, we used essential oil essences for aromatherapy in the bedroom. People in love can add new meaning to their romantic ways by choosing a fragrance that you only use during lovemaking. For him, patchouli; for her, sandalwood. If you use them only in the sacred bedroom, wherever you go in the world, those smells will remind you of your personal sanctuary and

A new commandment
I give you, that you love
one another.

∽ John 13:34

the delights you enjoy there together. Your special fragrance takes you to that level. Only use this scent in your sacred bedroom. It will become the scent of your sacred bedroom. A specific incense works well, too, as an exclusive cue to your sacred bedroom romance.

Gifts: Gifts are always appreciated, whether once a year or once a day. Little gifts remind us of past good times, favorite hobbies, profound events, and meditations we have shared together. Gifts can be souvenirs from special trips you have taken or a new item for the altar. On your next vacation, secretly bring home a pebble, leaf, or shells from the beach. Wrap the gift and leave it on your partner's pillow. The best gifts may be those you make yourself. Whatever you decide, let your gifts remind you and your partner of the greatest gift — love.

Hugs and kisses: Whenever you hug, close your eyes and imagine that there is a heart behind your heart. Picture it as a pink mother-of-pearl aura glowing inside your chest. When you hug, let the energy of love triple in your imagination. Fill your bodies with this supercharged energy of the heart. Imagine that each kiss is the spark of creation itself; your lips parting like the separation of the sexes when Adam and Eve were made in the image of God.

Love notes: Partners can place notes on each other's pillows, in briefcases, pockets, on a mirror, or in a brown-bag lunch. Your notes can be the familiar terms of affection, or reminders of love's sacred connection. Use simple words that convey stirring or evocative, even seductive, suggestions. Reaffirm in each other your divine qualities: "I love you as you express love in all you do." After reading your love notes, you may care to leave them on the altar for a time and include their messages in your sacred services.

Music: Make time to play mellow music, preferably instrumental, so the mind is not abducted by the pull of lyrics. Consider chants or a piece of classical music. (My wife and I favor "Eine Kleine Nachtmusik" by W. A. Mozart or Antonio Vivaldi's *The Four Seasons*.) Change the music every month or so as you become accustomed to it. Consider playing particular selections of music that you will only play in the bedroom, so they remind you of the delights and sanctity you experience there.

Yet a little sleep, a little slumber, a little folding of the hands to sleep.

꙳ Proverbs 6:10

Photos: Commemorate events from your life with carefully selected photos. Place a meaningful photo in a frame on your altar or elsewhere in the bedroom. You can place your wedding picture on your altar as well as some image that best symbolizes your union. Whenever you pray, you will be giving your relationship energy and a permanent home in your heart.

In order to welcome romance into our spiritual lives, we need to look beneath the flowers and favors. Life does not always foster the delights of romance or the privileges of being head over heels in love with our partner. When we are in love, no remedy is necessary. When we aren't, we have to recognize when the relationship is broken or perhaps in need of repair. The sacred bedroom is the perfect setting to play out the recommendations of counseling.

After the fireworks of courtship, we settle into the daily routine, and, if the relationship is to last, a deeper, more enduring love needs to grow. What is that love? How does it differ from being in love and the whirlwind fancies of romance? It is the highest love of all; a love that can be cultivated and practiced with intent in the sacred bedroom as everywhere. I call it "True Love," and it is the subject of the next section.

FINDING TRUE LOVE

We express love in many ways. We love our parents, siblings, partners, and friends, and sometimes manifest a spiritual love that our heroes and saints demonstrate even at the cost of their lives. The word confuses us because we apply it to so many things: I love ice cream. I love my classes. I love my dog, an organization, a political platform, a mathematical formula, or motorcycle. I love, I love, I love.

For most of us, falling in love is a brief rocket ship ride that we experience perhaps only once in life. If being in love were a permanent condition, how happy the world would be. But once we are in love with someone who returns that love, our egos sometimes get in the way. The ego wants only for self, so it reacts with

> In the spiritual marriage the union is like what we have when rain falls from the sky into a river or fount; all is water, for the rain that fell from heaven cannot be divided or separated from the water of the river.
>
> ∽ Teresa of Avila

shifting moods, selfish desires, and unrealistic expectations to that great enemy of romance: change.

People who stay together over the years develop an enduring, abiding love that allows them to adapt to conflict: Their love transcends the limitations of the word and approaches the eternal. Whether or not we are madly in love, we need this deeper, more constant love to sustain our relationships over the long run. True Love is a spiritual love based on selfless service to another that can withstand the changes and challenges of relationships. With True Love, you can transform your bedroom sanctuary into a mystical temple of love that you may never want to leave.

As the Indian sages say of Brahman (the Creator), you can liken love to a diamond. Turning it around in your hand, you will eventually see all the facets — but you can never see all the facets at once. The world's scriptures describe love in phrases of striking similarity: God-Is-Love is the universal message. Love has no beginning or end. It emanates from within the center of all thought. It is uncreated. It has neither a beginning nor an end. The Highest Power is the origin, the background, and the foreground of love. Love contains all of nature. It creates forever that which magnifies and reproduces itself endlessly.

When we seek out sacred places, we do so in order to feel closer to love. Thousands of books have been written on it, but expressing love is actually very simple, once you take away the analysis and the ego. You will know how to express love if you recall this fact, universally accepted throughout the world, that was discussed in chapter 1: Treat your partner as you would have him or her treat you. You can express love simply by feeling love and feeling loved by the Allness of love, which is the Creator — no one has to be present either to receive love from you or even to know how you are feeling in order for you to merge with love. Simply let it be and enjoy it. If you do have a partner in your life, in your bedroom you have a built-in workshop for love.

Our capacity to love is the great evidence that we are created in the divine image. No matter how we are feeling or thinking, we can free ourselves anytime from self-imposed emotional burdens through plain, honest givingness to our partners. We can lose

> Just as God is truly our Father, so also is God truly our Mother.
>
> ⁓ Julian of Norwich

ourselves in devotion to that person and forgive slights when we realize that the nourishing nectar of love comes from the simple spark that keeps our hearts beating — life itself. We are capable of great sacrifices, even the loss of our lives, in order to save or spare those we love.

Giving selflessly in a relationship when you are in a selfish mood is pretty tough. But the great benefit of expressing love for another is that, just for the moment, you can stop building walls around your heart and give yourself a rest. Giving to your partner frees you from stress. The time you spend loving another allows your heart to heal from the hurts when love was rejected.

The joy of lovers in love flows from the love bursting from the heart of the Creative Force — God-Is-Love — married inexorably to its creation, humankind. It is the heart behind the heart of love toward which I AM is always turning our heads. I AM draws you to I AM within yourself and your beloved. Lovers in love, giving selflessly in True Love, are trading in the commodity of God-Is-Love. Their delirious joy and excitement are the same described by the saints who experience spontaneous visions of the Divine.

True Love is more than an abstract idea. It is love in action. The evidence of love, projected through loving action, is the key to possessing it. Right action is the fourth principle in the Buddhist Eightfold Path. It is the basic principle of karma yoga. Karma, the law of cause and effect, stipulates that what we sow, so shall we reap. In a relationship, as in every aspect of our lives, we plant a seed with every word or deed. If we are planting seeds of demands, expectations, inflexibility, unforgivingness, vengefulness, manipulation, and dishonesty, this universal law, operating with the surety of physics, returns to us the fruits of those seeds.

We can discover True Love within us. Knowing True Love is more difficult to describe than the effervescent joys of being in love or romance. It may also be simpler, once you realize that, with all our ego-centered desires out of the way, True Love is our natural state. True Love is love the way the Creator loves. It is the key to lasting happiness because it is elemental and universal. It is the selfless caring for the partner, unconditionally, if your relationship were perfect. True Love is commitment and perseverance far

If I may trust the flattering truth of sleep, My dreams presage some joyful news at hand; My bosom's lord sits lightly in his throne; And all this day an unaccustom'd spirit Lifts me above the ground with cheerful thoughts.

∼ Shakespeare, *Romeo and Juliet*

Why do some people want to keep the Spirit (God) in the parlor while making love in the bedroom? The best sources seem to suggest that God likes bedrooms, too. In fact — can we possibly emphasize it enough? — God invented the bedroom's activity. So making love can celebrate God's creativity in our own design as human lovers.

 Dody H. Donnelly,
Radical Love

beyond romance and the excitement of courtship. True Love is forgiveness, again and again and again. It is compassion beyond judgment. Even partners who live together for years with no particular spark of being in love can practice True Love.

If what we feel for another is True Love, it supports romance, but is not dependent upon it. True Love is our individualized version of divine love; our demonstration of God-Is-Love from within us that is effortless once we understand it. Change can destroy romance; douse the fires of a love affair. But change is powerless against True Love. It is all in your attitude. Discovering ways in which you already unknowingly practice True Love shows you that you can live up to its fullness, especially in the sacred bedroom, where the setting is conducive to being your authentic self.

Whenever you enter the sacred bedroom, try to enter with love already blooming in your heart and leave all else outside the door. Enter your sacred bedroom anticipating its peace, stillness, and restfulness. This will help the Creator within you reveal love in your daily life. It will make the evidence of divine love visible. Whether we are alone in the sacred bedroom or sharing it with a partner, True Love permeates that holy space as surely and vibrantly as a flame of fire lights and heats a room. Bearing this in mind sets a stage in the heart for the appearance of True Love.

Think of yourself and your partner as vessels of True Love, opposing polarities that transcend your bodies and your personalities when you join together. Reach deeply within you, inside the core of your romantic feelings to that selfless, unchangeable God-Is-Love knowledge. Recall this reality often there, whether you are praying, meditating, making love, or just discussing how the day went. True Love is spiritual love that requires diligence and daily work to keep alive. It is holding the ego's demands at bay. It is also the vantage point from the highest realm of your consciousness to keep yourself in perspective, no matter what shape your love life is in.

The rest of your life can take on a new light by practicing True Love in your sacred bedroom experience. To practice and keep love in the sacred bedroom, and elsewhere, remember that love in every form emanates from the Divine. As you hover with your partner in the higher atmospheres of True Love, you are ready to apply another powerful concept in your sacred bedroom: the mystical bride and groom.

THE MYSTICAL BRIDE AND GROOM

A mystical alchemy occurs in the seemingly ordinary act of lovers joining in the private sanctuary of the bedroom. Bringing your divine masculine and feminine energies together commemorates the divine image in which we are made. Even in the haze of exhaustion at day's end, the two of you, being together, create a third energy, the unseen power of your union.

These powerful masculine and feminine forces underlie the workings of the universe. They are highly visible in the world around us, most obviously in the fact of gender on our planet — males and females that reproduce life itself through sex. The polarities of masculine and feminine are reflections of the push-pull between the moon and sun, the self and Spirit, darkness and light, giving and receiving.

Creation pours ceaselessly from the mystical unity of the divine masculine and feminine. Out of the joining of men and women comes new human beings: offspring perpetuating the gifts of life and love through the union of hearts and bodies. In the sacred bedroom, the mystical power of this principle can be thought of as a charged coil that changes the creative dynamics of partnerships. Its beauty can be admired through the simple awareness of the power of gender. This polarity also holds true for gay men and women, as the masculine or feminine qualities will be stronger in one partner than in the other.

We can appreciate the beauty of this polarity through the concept of the "mystical bride and groom." Also known as the "mystical marriage," this ancient concept can help us realize that we are more like our Creator than we think we are. It appears among the Egyptians, Romans, and the Greeks, who knew it as *hieros gamos*. It is also present in Hindu, Buddhist, and Taoist teachings.

The mystical marriage is also applied to the relationship between individuals and the Creator, as expressed in Isaiah, for

> In sleep, what difference is there between Solomon and a fool?
>
>   A proverb

Bedtime Story

The Great Bed of Ware was referred to in Shakespeare's *Twelfth Night*. It started out in 1570 at a monstrous 18$\frac{1}{2}$ feet by 12 feet. It was later reduced to a 12 by 12 square and ended up in various inns, where eighteenth- and nineteenth-century businessmen used it for spectacular, sometimes group, seductions.

example, where the Chosen People are identified as the "virgin bride" of Jehovah: "For your Maker is your Husband, the Lord of Hosts is His name; and the Holy One of Israel is your Redeemer, the God of the whole earth He is called." (Isaiah 54:5) In the Bible, there are dozens of such references to humankind as the bride of deity.

This principle is exemplified in the mating of the masculine and feminine forces in romance: boy finds girl; boy loses girl; boy finds girl — and vice versa. The desire for that perfect "soul mate," operating in the very core of our beings, is a reflection of our desire to reunite with the Creator. What stirs us about romantic stories is the image of God (male and female aspects) at the core of consciousness that drives us unceasingly to unite with the beloved. It is the story of Isis and Osiris, Ariadne and Dionysus, Romeo and Juliet, Tony and Maria, Tristan and Iseult, Luke Skywalker and Princess Leia. It is the operative force in every fairy tale of prince or princess.

Our masculine and feminine polarity reflects the most powerful creative force in the universe. It even exist within us as individuals. We have an inner male and inner female, one of which tends to be dominant in how we view and express ourselves in the world. In the sacred bedroom, we can strengthen our relationship and bring clarity and power to our self-image by balancing the masculine and feminine forces within us. Balance will help us dispel gender assumptions and prejudices as we adopt an enlightened attitude toward the divine aspects of ourselves and our partner. (See the "Balancing the Masculine and Feminine Within" exercise on page 115.)

Balancing the masculine and feminine forces within you can help you become aware of powers you never thought you had. When you enter the bedroom at night, before you kick off your shoes, take a moment to honor the divine masculine and feminine principles that you embody. Take a deep bow. Whenever you and your partner greet each other in the sacred bedroom, regard the sacred bride and groom within you. Discover your intrinsic divinity, and honor it in your sacred bedroom through celebration and ritual.

Balancing the Masculine and Feminine Within

Discover new confidence, strength, self-respect, and inner security by reviewing how you react when you are in your masculine mode and when in your feminine mode. Men and women both need to acknowledge the presence of these opposites within them. During meditation, consider the following qualities and descriptions one at a time. List on paper those qualities you seem to lack, and spend a day discovering and using those missing qualities. In this way, you will achieve balance.

Masculine	Feminine
Initiator	Follower
Aggressor	Receptor
Builder	Decorator
Defender	Protector
Provider	Nurturer
Speaker	Listener
Reasoning	Intuitive
Objective	Subjective
Mental	Emotional
Bridegroom	Bride

RITUALS FOR PARTNERS

Displaying sacred objects is an excellent way to turn the bedroom into a sacred space. However, you need to create new daily habits in order to practice a more sacred life. Habits are difficult to form, especially regarding the abstract nature of spirituality, so we need a mechanism known in every spiritual tradition, from Anglican to Zoroastrian: the use of ritual and ceremony.

Rituals help us fully live what we believe in our hearts by creating the outward evidence for what we think. Without the visible demonstration, there is only the idea, however noble it may be. Like enthusiasm, ideas can fade in time, but the use of ritual can keep the spirit of the idea fresh in our minds.

W. Brugh Joy, M.D., author of *Joy's Way*, once said, "There's a part of your psyche that doesn't know the difference between

He fashioneth their
hearts alike.

∽   Psalms 33:15

Who is awake, who
creates lovely dreams,
when man is
lost in sleep?
That Person through
whom all things live,
beyond whom none can
go; pure, powerful,
immortal spirit.

🙶 The Upanishads

a ritual and an actual event." By going through the motions of a ritual, a part of your mind accepts and believes the symbolism you attribute to it. If you consecrate your altar by lighting a candle, folding your hands, and speaking prayers, your mind accepts that your altar is consecrated. Moreover, your mind will accept that your bedroom is sacred, that you, yourself, are made in the image of God, and that making love is part of the Creator's creative model. Without ritual, the mind merely entertains a possibility. Using ritual, the mind believes a concept as truth, because we have demonstrated it in action.

Rituals in religious services give many people comfort, but cause others to glaze over in numbness from what becomes, for them, meaningless repetition. Rituals in a church service formalize the purposes of the service through gestures, prayers, and readings, making physical the abstract concepts of faith. It is up to us to bring that meaning to life in our hearts, rather than merely go through the motions.

In simple terms, a ritual is a prescribed ceremony repeated for a specific intention, using meaningful words, actions, and objects that symbolize concepts, teachings, or events. But rituals are part of our daily lives whether we realize it or not, and not all of them are religious. For example, when Dad does the cooking during a backyard barbecue, it may be a ritual reenactment of the primal provider who brought mastodon steaks home to roast on the community fire. Secular holidays are especially dense with rituals. Taking Mom out to dinner on Mother's Day and *not* working on Labor Day are rituals. We practice other rituals getting ready for work in the morning, preparing for a date, or before stepping up to the plate during a baseball game. Many of us practice rituals before going to bed at night, such as reading a few pages in a book, and after getting up in the morning, such as throwing open the curtains and greeting the day.

Using rituals in our lives makes us feel good. They connect life in the outer world to the testing ground of meaning in the heart. They help us remember what it is that we love because they are outward demonstrations of our beliefs, giving us spiritual stability in this distracting world. Practicing rituals with others connects us socially and spiritually in the community. Rituals and ceremonies, in fact, help us become better acquainted with our authentic self, that spiritual self that returns when we practice them. They add the practice to what we preach and can help firm up the foundation of romance. Through ritual we can fine-tune our practice of True Love.

For many, religious ceremonies tend to follow rigid rules and adhere to minute-to-minute schedules. Over time, they can seem wooden. In the sacred bedroom you can be creative in the use of rituals, because they are only for you and your partner. Your rituals can be whatever they need to be in order to outwardly demonstrate the feeling that you are one with God-Is-Love. They should help satisfy your need to feel close to the sacred. They should help you sustain your goals, your spiritual ideals, and your momentum for keeping True Love alive in your heart. You can change or update your rituals and ceremonies at any time, and keep the meaning fresh.

The best bedroom ceremonies are the ones you create yourself for your particular needs and situation. They need not follow strict rules but can follow loose guidelines. Your sacred bedroom rituals can be simple or elaborate, and you may personalize them with any of the following traditions:

- Wear a piece of clothing that has some meaningful color or design. (This can be as simple as a scarf or neck piece, a shirt or blouse, or prayer shawl.)

- Sit before your altar during your ritual. (This symbolizes presenting yourself to the Highest Power. Sit in a chair, or on the floor in the yogic lotus position or on a sturdy pillow made for meditation.)

- Say a few words to declare a ritual's purpose, such as, "We join together in this ritual to consecrate our sacred bedroom." Use any prayer, affirmation, or blessing that has special meaning for you.

- Light a candle. (Light symbolizes consciousness, understanding, and awareness.)

Romance, like a ghost,
eludes touching.
It is always
where you were,
not where you are.

       G. W. Curtis,
Lotus-Eating

- Ring a bell. (The pure tone of a bell clears the mental and emotional spaces and attunes you to the frequency of higher consciousness.)

- Slowly take three deep breaths. (Breath makes you one with the rhythm of the universe. Breath breathes Spirit in, discord out.)

- Meditate. (A moment of meditation before your ritual helps you focus on the intended purpose of the ritual.)

Be creative in designing your rituals and be aware of purpose. In *Sacred World: The Shambhala Way to Gentleness, Bravery, and Power*, Jeremy and Karen Hayward write, "Even the seemingly trivial aspects of life — the clothes you wear and how you wear them, the food you eat, or the mug you drink out of — can contribute to the overall sacredness of your life when you appreciate the inner meaning of ritual."

Remember that no ritual word, object, or action is meant to substitute for what it represents. This often happens in sacred and secular rituals alike, in which a ritual has been performed so often, for so many years, people no longer remember what it is for. Longtime habits have led to worshipping the symbols, such as statues or icons, rather than the spiritual truth they symbolize. For this reason, it makes sense to change or vary your rituals periodically so you can keep them fresh and meaningful.

As your personal refuge within the house, the sacred bedroom can be used to experiment with a host of rituals. You and your partner can explore them in order to deepen your spiritual practice, discover the masculine and feminine energies within you, or simply to add a sacred dimension to your romance.

Here are some rituals specifically designed to perform with your partner. Again, open your ceremonies by lighting a candle and sounding a bell, followed by a moment of deep breathing and meditation. Close with a bell tone and, finally, extinguish the flame.

Honoring each other: Couples can create quality time by periodically formalizing their respect for one another through ritual. There is no better place to do this than in the bedroom — the

> It is God who arrangeth marriages....
> Those whom he hath once joined he joineth forever.
>
> ❧ Guru Nanak, prophet of the Sikh religion

single most powerful symbol of your partnership. Honoring each other in this way is akin to renewing your vows — whatever vows you live by, whether or not you are married. In such a ritual, couples can write into the service as many elements of their relationship as they wish.

For this ritual, be seated in front of the altar and face each other. Raise your hands and place your palms together. Look into each other's eyes. Ring the bell after each statement is read or recited.

Together: "I sit before the throne of I AM THAT I AM to honor the divine image within my partner and myself."

Place your hands on your knees or fold them on your lap. You may read a passage from scripture, a vow, or a prayer of gratitude. It may be a statement of conviction about your relationship in the future, or a restating of your marriage vows. You may express gratitude for an accomplishment or some milestone reached. Use this model for an honoring ceremony of your own design:

Partner #1: "I honor you, [name], for the divine image within you and in the name of True Love by which I care for you."

Partner #2: "I honor you, [name], for the divine image within you and in the name of True Love by which I care for you."

Now, meditate for a moment more on the meaning of these statements and then both of you read or recite

Together: "We commit our love, time, energy, and resources to the success of our relationship, in accomplishing our mutual goals, keeping our household holy, and our bedroom sacred, for the greater outpouring of love to all every day."

Naturally, one can also celebrate life's rites of passage — a promotion at work, an honor bestowed — anywhere in the house. But in the sacred bedroom, this format is especially adaptable for any form of honor because of the privacy and the beneficial presence of the altar.

The Lord God, all-pervading and omnipresent, dwells in the heart of all beings. Full of grace, he ultimately gives liberation to all creatures by turning their faces toward himself.

∽ Svetasvatara Upanishad

When you are in
love with someone,
you do indeed see them
as a divine being.
Now, suppose that is
what they truly are
and that your eyes
have by your beloved
been opened.
Through a tremendous
outpouring of psychic
energy in total devotion
and worship for
this other person,
who is respectively god
or goddess, you realize,
by total fusion and
contact, the
divine center in them.
At once it bounces back
to you and you
discover your own.

꙳ Alan Watts,
Play to Live

If you wish to express gratitude for some particular blessing in your life, include a statement such as

Partner #1: "[Name], you have brought honor to our house through your [promotion, raise, victory, et cetera]. Let us express gratitude to the Creative Force for the talents and circumstances that have made this possible."

Together: "Gratitude keeps the doors of our hearts open for new opportunities and blessings. We thank the Lord for life."

In your meditation, you can contemplate how your accomplishments tie into your overarching spiritual goals. Remember that in the bedroom sanctuary, seated before the altar, you can claim any experience as part of your intimacy with the Divine. If you wish, you can incorporate the Japanese tradition of a bow. Serve each other a cup of tea. Seal the ritual with a ritual hug.

Sealing a pact: Whenever you and your partner reach some special agreement or make an important promise, you can seal it in a bedroom ritual. This could involve anything from agreeing to change a behavior to starting a new financial plan. It could revolve around visiting each other's families, or simply be a promise to spend more time together. Before your ceremony, write out the basic statement of your agreement or pact. Follow the preliminary formalities in which you honor the presence of the Divine, light a candle, and meditate briefly. Now read or recite a prepared statement such as the following:

Together: "I am a thread in the fabric of eternity. There is no more important activity than spending an hour each evening alone with my partner, [name], free of worldly distractions."

Seal the pact by feeding each other an apple, or placing a symbolic object, such as a gem, stone, shell, et cetera, on your altar as a reminder. Repeat the ritual daily if the commitment is especially difficult to accomplish. If you fail to honor the commitment, discuss it again outside the bedroom and evaluate the reason. Forgiveness is essential in order to move forward. Repeating the ritual gives each of you another chance to bring the commitment into reality in concrete terms. If you wish, rewrite your basic statement to keep the intention fresh.

Forgiving: Formalizing the act of forgiveness through ritual is one of the most important uses of ritual, because forgiveness is so bound up in the fickle realm of the emotions. We can say we forgive, but feelings of hurt and betrayal can linger or embed themselves deeply, emerging again later. A good time for this ritual is after a breech of trust or some unfortunate argument.

For this ritual, place an unlit candle between you, or on the front of your altar, and complete your breathing cycle.

Partner #1: "[Name], I am sorry I failed you through my actions, and ask your forgiveness in the name of I AM THAT I AM."

Partner #2: "[Name], I do forgive you, and in this forgiveness help our trust to deepen and our commitment to be strengthened."

Together: "We light this flame for the renewal of True Love on a foundation of trust and forgiveness."

Meditate further on the commitment (not on the failure), and complete the ritual with a hug. Blow out the flame, but leave the candle at the front of the altar for some agreed-upon period of time.

Lovemaking: Next to our capacity to love, our sexuality may be the single most fundamental connection we have to the creative forces of the Divine. We will look more closely at sexuality in the next chapter, but the sacred act of lovemaking lends itself especially well to ritual and celebration.

A simple but powerful ritual to use before making love begins with partners seated before the altar facing each other. Whenever you make love, you can enhance the experience by beginning with a meditation for focusing your thoughts and calming your emotions. Place a candle on each side of the bed, if you wish (being careful of fire), and light incense that you will only use during lovemaking. Ring the bell, symbolizing the sound at the center of

To love means to decide independently to live with an equal partner, and to subordinate oneself to the formation of a new subject, a "we."

∽ Fritz Kunkel, *Let's Be Normal*

all creation. Place the palms of your hands together and dedicate your lovemaking by reading or reciting

Together: "We honor the divine creative force as we join together in this mystical marriage of body and soul. With True Love and gratitude, I dedicate my body and mind for your pleasure, consecrate my energy for your healing, and open my heart in the approval of the Creator."

Enjoy lovemaking together in the freedom of knowing that in making love in the spirit of love, you are displaying the spirit of creation itself. Write a prayer that consecrates your lovemaking as a sacred experience.

Dedicate your lovemaking to the causes of love, healing, and even world peace! Invite Spirit to be present with you, to envelop you, to keep and bless you during your encounter.

Conceiving children: Ritual can help any situation, even conceiving children. Parents know that each soul is unique. They see the uncanny personality differences between newborn babies, who seem to enter life with preexisting attitudes, urges, and tendencies.

When trying to conceive a child, partners may request a special soul. In a relaxed, meditative state, discuss why you want to have the child. Discuss what you can offer and your commitment to rearing the child in a loving atmosphere, and not for artificial reasons, such as salvaging your relationship. Rededicate your love for one another with the "Honoring Each Other" ritual above or the "Commitment" ritual below.

Now read or recite a prayer for conception, and build into that prayer your commitment and love for each other as well as for the child about to be conceived. Consider an affirmation such as

In the name of I AM THAT I AM, we invite a special soul to be our child, one for whom we can offer the best love and guidance for his or her spiritual mission.

Affirming commitment: Whether you sealed your partnership with a formal marriage ceremony or not, you can add the sacred dimension to your long-term commitment to each other. In

If thou must love me,
let it be for nought
Except for love's
sake only.

∾ **Elizabeth Barrett Browning,**
Sonnets from the Portuguese

this ritual, you will use a bowl of water; if possible, use a crystal bowl, to enhance the value of your experience. Float rose petals in the water and place the bowl between you. Both of you then grasp the bowl and, while holding it, read or recite your vows, prayers, or statement of commitment.

As both of you hold the bowl, take turns sipping the water. You can also acquire a two-handled cup, the *coupe de mariage,* from which couples in France drink a wedding toast. Take turns drinking from the cup as you both hold it. The marriage cup symbolizes the union of two lives — partners sipping life as one. The two-handled cup or crystal bowl symbolizes your partnership and can be given a place on your altar as a reminder of your commitment together.

Cleaning: Another bedroom ritual that offers lasting benefits may come as a surprise: cleaning. In *The Temple in the House,* architect Anthony Lawlor writes, "The simplest, most direct method of creating sacredness in everyday surroundings is cleaning. I know this activity is usually relegated to the realm of drudgery, but it can become a practical means of infusing consciousness into your surroundings. Sacredness is experienced in the qualities of purity, orderliness, balance, and renewal. All of these are achieved through cleaning."

Set a regular time each week or month for cleaning your bedroom thoroughly. Make it fun. Open the windows, let the sun shine in, play music, and visualize the positive *ch'i* flowing throughout the room. Involve your partner or enlist your children to help you. After each cleaning reconsecrate your sacred bedroom according to the instructions in chapter 2.

Try to be mindful of the higher purpose in cleaning. Enjoy the moment. Meditate on the brush strokes, the wiping, scrubbing, mopping, as love in action. Think of cleaning as karma yoga practice in which every action is positive, performed with positive intent. Being conscious of the sacred while performing such tasks as mundane as cleaning will help you be more conscious of the sacred in other acts that you perform in your bedroom: prayer, worship, meditation, sleep and dreaming, and sexual intimacy, the subject of the next chapter.

Every form of human life is romantic.

    ❧ T. W. Higginson,
A Plea for Culture

Recipes for the Sacred Bedroom

Romantic interludes: Try a dish of strawberries served with champagne or make ice cream sundaes for two.

Aphrodisiac: Make an aloe cooler by combining in a blender, until smooth, $1/2$ cup aloe vera juice, 1 teaspoon of spirulina (blue-green algae), chunks of frozen banana, and 1 cup of pineapple chunks with juice.

Love vanquishes time. To lovers, a moment can be eternity, eternity can be the tick of a clock.

∾ Mary Parrish, "All the Love in the World"

6

Global Warming

I am a full-grown Bride
I must to my lover's side!

— Mechthild of Magdeburg

The bedroom is home to sexuality, our most pleasurable physical experience, and one of our most direct connections to Spirit. We can rejoice in the divine aspects of sex in the sacred bedroom through knowledge of the hidden energies of lovemaking. We can also use the lessons of sacred sexuality to live more peacefully in our day-to-day lives.

THE COSMIC DANCE

Sex is one of the most powerful and mysterious forces of life. In its essence, it links humankind together in that most joyful act in which partners passionately join their bodies until released in the lightning flash of orgasm. The hidden scope of sex contains the essence of divine creativity going back to the creation of heaven and earth. For this reason sex may be the most life-affirming experience of the sacred bedroom. It is also the most neglected and misunderstood component of our spiritual life.

During sex, the forces of divine creativity are intensely evident. No other act that two people perform results in the physical pleasure of orgasm. No other act between two people can result in the crown of creation: the conception and birth of a new human being. Perhaps in no other human experience, with the exception of agony, do we call out the Lord's name with such heartfelt power and conviction: "Oh God!"

At first blush, we must accept some connection between sex and Spirit. After all, mating is a natural mirror of the Creator. We need to consecrate sex and include it in our concept of the sacred, just as we do prayer or performing selfless acts for others.

> Sexuality is too powerful a force to deny or put aside on one hand; but it is also too powerful a force to let run our lives on the other. So what shall we do? We must consecrate it.
>
> ∽ Bede Griffiths

Genesis tells us that by our very maleness and femaleness, we share in the image of God. In Eden, we were, at first, unashamed. We can reclaim this state of innocence in the bedroom through sacred sexuality. The difficulty we have in learning this lesson is the emphasis we place on the outer world, with all its toys and appearances, and our neglect of the inner meaning of our bedroom activities. It is also due to the failure of our religious institutions to teach us about the sacred aspects of our sexual nature.

According to Georg Feuerstein in *Sacred Sexuality,* "sacred sexuality is...about communing or identifying with the ultimate Reality, the Divine. This is a decisive distinction. For the spiritual practitioner, sexual intercourse is an opportunity to encounter the sacred dimension, which surpasses the individual man or woman just as it surpasses all other manifest forms. The bliss arising from the sexual union is not orgasmic pleasure but the innate delight of the primordial Androgyne, the ultimate Male/Female, the God/Goddess."

Many of the great religions of humankind do not segregate sexuality from spirituality. They embrace both as equally important gifts from God, and that is no less true in our Western traditions.

The male and female combination mysteriously contained in the image of God is stated in Genesis. But reading further in the Bible, one sees that the history of Judaism, and Christianity that followed, was shaped by many events centered around the bedroom.

Read about the idolatrous cults to which the Israelites fell victim along the way. Consider fifteen-year-old Queen Esther, who saved her nation more than once in the bedroom of King Ahasuerus. Bathsheba and Delilah changed the courses of nations in their bedrooms. While David was out of town, Absalom tried to assert his right to the throne by publicly bedding 10 of Dad's concubines in full view of the populace. Solomon would eventually have 700 wives and 300 concubines.

The books of Genesis, Numbers, and Deuteronomy contain many detailed laws regarding bedchamber behavior, but the Song of Songs is a celebration of the divine nature of sexual love. The Old Testament asserts that sexual union is the supreme divine gift — man and wife passionately fulfilling the covenants and laws of the prophets. Kabbalah, or mystical Judaism, contains teachings on the symbolic masculine and feminine and applies them to every part of the universe, to God, the mind, and man and woman.

Kabbalists teach that the body and mind are one and that we should not mortify the flesh. It also teaches that God contains both male and female. If sexual partners meditate on the tetragrammaton (YHWH = Yahweh = the holy name of God = I AM THAT I AM) while making love "all consciousness of self disappears."

In *The Shambhala Guide to Kabbalah and Jewish Mysticism,* Perle Besserman writes, "Contemporary female Kabbalists are few, but it is through them that the breach between male and female will eventually be repaired. Thus sexual intercourse is a great spiritual teacher. Satisfaction is only achieved if the man discovers the female principle within himself, and the woman discovers the male principle within herself. In sexual union the divine unity of heaven is restored."

Kabbalah freely identifies the masculine and feminine as aspects of the divine image. It further declares that union with God is the goal of the spiritual path. The classic mystical *Zohar* offers much to instruct us in the sacred bedroom.

In *9 1/2 Mystics,* Rabbi Herbert Weiner writes, "The *Zohar* sees nothing unspiritual about examining the human body, and in particular the sex act, as a paradigm of the hidden spiritual universe from which all existence draws its life."

The soft tenderness of the delicate blossom gently presses against the tips of my fingers, offering the warmth of ecstasy surrendered by the dearest face held between the palms of a lover's hands.

— Swami Premananda, *The Sanctity of the Senses*

Georg Feuerstein, in *Sacred Sexuality,* also paraphrases the *Zohar,* saying that "sexual pleasure brings delight to the feminine power of the Divine. Moreover, because of the perfect parallelism or homology between microcosm and macrocosm, a couple's sexual pleasure was thought to even magnify the peace in the world."

As an exercise, try thinking of the Highest Power during your next sexual experience. Sound boring? Then you are not trying hard enough to understand that God gives bliss in every language, even the language of sex. Sexuality is part of who you are. Your partner, your helpmate, is a gift who possesses within him or her the united masculine and feminine principles: one who can lead you to discovering the androgynous reality of your Divine Self.

Christian literature rarely connects sexuality directly to the sacred, except perhaps by extension, for example, when Jesus quoted the Old Testament that no man should put asunder that which God has joined together. Jesus said little directly on the subject of sex, speaking more often about how people should treat each other. He preached not to commit adultery in the heart or in deed, yet to love one's neighbor as oneself — a code that, if applied by spouses and lovers, could smooth out the wrinkles in any sacred bedroom.

Prominent religious commentator and former Roman Catholic nun Karen Armstrong writes in *A History of God,* "There is no human activity which is alien to God; even the sexuality repressed by the Church is manifest in the passion of Jesus himself."

Many modern Christian thinkers, if not the church fathers themselves, are taking a more enlightened approach to some of the canonical assumptions that were made for Christians in the first few centuries of its existence.

In *The Coming of the Cosmic Christ* theologian and former Roman Catholic priest Matthew Fox offers a refreshing view that "lovemaking (as distinct from 'having sex') is Christ meeting Christ. Love beds are altars. People are temples encountering temples, the holy of holies receiving the holy of holies. Wings of cherubim and seraphim beat to the groans and passions of human lovers, for the cosmic powers are there to enhance the celebration."

The ecstatic visions of many Christian mystics have been

> There is no fear in love; but perfect love casts out fear.
>
> ∾ 1 John 4:18

likened to sexual experiences. Hildegard von Bingen, for example, compared the Trinity to three aspects of sexual intercourse: strength, desire, and the act itself. Theresa of Avila's ecstatic infatuation with Jesus included a series of visions in which the Nazarene showed himself to her in physical form. He showed himself to her, she said, to cure her of her romantic love for him, to ignite spiritual love, True Love, which then guided her for the rest of her life.

Many others wrote of their ecstasy while beholding the Lord. One can look to the mystics and saints of every religion to find eloquent descriptions of the ecstasy of union with the Divine. In our highest, most enlightened sexual experiences, we receive glimpses of the eternal ecstasy that the saints and adepts achieved through True Love alone.

When fully understood, sex belongs to Spirit even though we use our bodies to express it. It is, to me, a mistake to amputate sex from our spiritual identities, because it is a natural part of how we are made. Matthew Fox writes in *One River, Many Wells,* "Sex is already sacred, for it is a part of the glory of the universe."

Islam, as well, connects sexuality with Spirit. It is well known that much of the Qur'an came to Muhammad in dreams, during which the angel Gabriel instructed him. The holy book of Islam contains many teachings on sexuality, taking for granted that sex is a sacred part of human life. It urges a man to utter a prayer prior to having sex, and then to concentrate on achieving maximum pleasure for himself and his partner. In the Sunna tradition, celibacy is forbidden and "the whole world is to be enjoyed." Though severely patriarchal in its orientation, Islam once had several teaching manuals on sexual love and its connection to Spirit. The lone surviving volume, *The Perfumed Garden,* is sometimes compared to the *Kama Sutra.*

These three traditions, all of which sprung from Abraham's calling, point to the inherent divinity of sexuality. Partners uniting in sex demonstrate two aspects of the image of God simply by their joining: expressions of love and the merging of the masculine and feminine into one as the mystical bride and groom. Add True Love, and you identify with the Creator in four dimensions — spiritual,

> When two people who are passionately, even madly...in love; when each wants most to receive what the other most wants to give — at the moment of their mutual climax, it is impossible to say whether the experience is more physical or spiritual, or whether they sense themselves as two or as one. The moment is ecstatic because at that moment they stand outside...themselves in the melded oneness of the Absolute.
>
> ✒ Huston Smith

mental, emotional, and physical — declaring I AM THAT I AM in ecstasy; love, and devotion to another.

Enlightened lovers in love play out the cosmic dance in Divine creative union, pulsating to the rhythm of the most profound, fundamental force in the universe. Many people rush through the experience, overlooking the grand scope for a momentary thrill that has no reflection in the mirror. Such experiences have no memory and serve little purpose other than to give the nervous system a brief jolt.

Sex in love can transport us to a rare and magnificent state of mind. Everyone achieves this consciousness during sex to some degree, depending upon the lovers' awareness. It is a plane of awareness that approaches God consciousness. With a higher awareness of enlightened sex in True Love, we can achieve what sacred sex teacher Margo Anand calls "sky dancing," after Yeshe Tsogyal, an enlightened Buddhist woman in eighth-century Tibet known as "Sky Dancer."

In *Sacred Sexuality* Georg Feuerstein writes, "Sacred sexuality is about recovering our authentic being, which knows bliss beyond mere pleasurable sensations. It is a special form of communication, even communion, that fills us with awe and stillness."

Lovemaking should seem natural for people, as a relaxing, meditative communion between two souls in the sacred light of the Creator and the blessings of the prophets. But there are imposing social forces that complicate our enjoyment of sex in a spiritual light. In addition to sexual taboos in some religions, the artificial world, specifically the illusion factory of the media, keeps lovemaking earthbound.

The bedroom should be thought of as a temple, where honest expressions of love, emotion, hope, heartbreak, triumph, sexual desire, and contentment bring the soul to the surface. The soul grows in brief spurts during our peak experiences of honest intimacy with our true feelings — and what we do about them when we are at our most vulnerable. This is when that authentic self that beamed through a summer's day in childhood sits comfortably in the heart and approaches God most closely. In your sacred bedroom, with all your artificial guards down, you can contact the

In winter I get up at night
And dress by yellow
candle-light.
In summer, quite the
other way,
I have to go
to bed by day.

～ Robert Louis Stevenson,
Bed in Summer

primal spark of creative imagination and innocence. You naturally drift toward conscious knowledge of the best you there is, wearing no masks, no costumes, on the body or the mind. Riding the tide of sexual expression with a pure heart and True Love as the only garment is a key to being truly free.

One can enjoy a deeper, more sacred experience of sex without having to master exotic techniques, although some study can be helpful. Awareness of the energies and sanctity of sex can help you be aware of the change in your consciousness. Just knowing its symbolic and literal parallels to the Creator's master blueprint can help make it sacred for you and your partner.

Little in life is more thrilling than the spontaneous, unbridled passion of two lovers devouring each other in a gale of fevered kisses. But you can transform that brief experience of sex and bring it into your life of sacred activity by cultivating planned, controlled sessions led by and concluding with meditation and prayer. The unbridled passion does not suffer. Guided with the bridle of the Divine, sex can open an entirely new realm of experience in your sacred bedroom.

The idea is to direct your passion like wind in a sail, rather than firing it like a Roman candle. Taking your time will give you the space in which to practice selfless giving during this normally self-pleasuring act. Letting its energies patiently build can introduce you to a new world of pleasure, one that is congruent with the image and laws of God, and bring you to heights of joy you never knew existed. This is the difference between spilling water from one glass to another, versus pouring the water: Nothing is lost when you pour. The pour can last and last as you pay out and take in each other's energies.

LIGHTNING PLANET

A view from space of earth's cloudy mantle reveals thousands of lightning strikes per second, like tiny flashbulbs flickering around the globe. That is how lovers might appear, illuminating the night with the fire of sexual union; a planet alive with the shimmer of life ecstatically begetting life.

Wild Nights – Wild Nights!
Were I with thee
Wild Nights should be
Our luxury!

Futile – the Winds –
To a Heart in port –
Done with the Compass –
Done with the Chart!

Rowing in Eden –
Ah, the Sea!
Might I but moor –
Tonight –
In Thee!

     Emily Dickinson,
The Complete Poems,
No. 249

When sex is imminent, the mind is crystal clear and the body sings. Tenderness overwhelms the emotions. For those in love, sex brims over into unity without inhibition, souls floating on swells of ecstasy.

Others rush to orgasm in a New York minute or choke with expectations and fears. Whatever our experience, when we make love we achieve an altered state of consciousness that is eclipsed by the physical sensations. Our awareness of that state depends upon our understanding of the subtle dynamics of sex. But we can deepen the experience and discover the sacred properties of sex by expanding our awareness of its hidden energies.

The world offers a vast library of books on sexual techniques that explore exotic positions, cures for sexual dysfunction, and ways of extending orgasm. The exotic "pillow books" of the East sit side by side with the mechanical "how-tos" of the West. *The Sacred Bedroom* looks beyond body positions and techniques, however, to focus on our inner experience, refine our attitudes toward pleasure, and show how sexuality connects with the Being who created sex in the first place.

What do we need to know to experience sex in a more sacred way? There is much one can study from the Eastern cultures. For our Western sensibilities and habits, perhaps less is more. We can benefit greatly if we understand a few key concepts that can help us be aware of that altered state of consciousness that occurs during sex. Although in the West sex manuals focus almost universally on the physical, there are several sources of sexual wisdom from the East that can help you welcome sacred sex into your sacred bedroom life.

Of the many traditions to choose from, I suggest that you consider some powerful concepts from three ancient traditions regarding sexuality: Taoist, Hindu, and Buddhist.

Spilling and Pouring

We can learn much about sacred sex from Taoist philosophy, which embraces the union of the masculine and feminine in the symbol of yin (feminine) and yang (masculine), perfect harmony expressed through the union of opposites. Taoists see everything

---

Sex is regarded in Judaism as a powerful force. At its highest spiritual level, sexual intercourse symbolizes the union between God and the shekinah — the feminine aspect — and thus produces Divine harmony.

 Sara Isaacson,
Principles of Jewish Spirituality

in terms of yin and yang (see the illustration in chapter 1, page 25). To them, the symbol of the white and black swirls, with a dot of each present in the other, represents the oneness of the Way (the Tao). Taoists believe that in sexual union the Divine is achieved as these two great forces join, and that the man and woman exchange these complementary energies through their bodies. In Taoism, the bedroom is not just a place to sleep and have sex, but a temple in which heaven and earth themselves join in the sacred union of the partners.

Taoists believe that sex is a ballet of energy, specifically *ch'i,* (discussed in chapter 2). You may recall that *ch'i* is the invisible energy that circulates freely throughout the universe, through our communities, homes, and rooms. But *ch'i* circulates in our bodies as well. *Ch'i* can be intentionally cultivated in the body in many ways without the use of sex (e.g., tai chi chuan, chi kung, and other arts). But the Taoists believe that sexual energy is actually supercharged *ch'i* that can be refined, controlled, amplified, circulated within the body, and shared between partners during sex.

Taoists explain that the altered state of consciousness achieved during sex accompanies changes in the nervous and circulatory systems. Sexual *ch'i,* they maintain, rises from the sexual organs through invisible channels, called meridians, to the head. Our ability to perceive the resulting exquisite and subtle elevation in consciousness depends on the depth of our awareness of body and energy. You can expand your awareness and use of this energy through various exercises, some of which are included in the next section.

Expanding your awareness of the hidden dynamics and subtle energies makes all the difference between mere copulation and enlightened lovemaking. Add to sex the ingredient of True Love, and we can lift our sights above the clouds of unrealistic desires and ignorance of the body, and take part, smiling, in the cosmic impulse by which we were created.

Whatever we do with our bodies during the act itself, we need to realize that a host of experiences, energies, merging of consciousness, and a tug of war in the heart — pleasing you vs. pleasing me — are also taking place. We can clear the decks for a purer

> Once upon a time I dreamed I was a butterfly. I was conscious only of following my fancies as a butterfly and was unaware of my individuality as a butterfly. Suddenly I was awakened and there I lay, myself again. Now I do not know whether I was a man dreaming I was a butterfly or whether I am a butterfly now dreaming I am a man.
>
> ∽ Chuang-tzu

experience, however, if we subordinate our expectations and fears of sex to a conscious effort to express True Love. We can then realize sex as a sacred act that transcends the body. With this awareness, sex becomes a sacred act that symbolically mimics the heart, mind, and image of God.

Ch'i energy has a dual nature, that of the yin (feminine) and yang (masculine). The ch'i we possess shifts between the two, depending on our attitudes and how we react to experiences. However, with sexual stimulation, men generate yang ch'i and women yin. The female's sexual response is inward, slow to arouse, rising and falling in waves. She is unhurried to conclude lovemaking. The male is fiery, outward, urgent to conclude with ejaculation.

Taoists give the starring role to the female during sex. Men learn to understand her nature, to cater to her pleasure, cultivate her sexual power, and partake of her powerful yin energy. Men also learn techniques of semen retention — the intentional deferring of ejaculation, which not only prolongs lovemaking, but retains for the man his powerful yang energy that is lost when he ejaculates. To many in the West, the idea of consciously withholding ejaculation amounts to forfeiting joy in sex. However, the Taoists, and people of other cultures who possess this knowledge, show that deeper pleasure is heightened and prolonged. The male is able to have sex more the way a woman does, enjoying hours of lovemaking without losing his vigor. Sacred sex becomes an ocean voyage rather than a brief swim. It becomes an extended experience in which couples can commune with the Divine.

If your sex life is everything you wish it to be, there is no point, as the saying goes, in fixing it if it is not broken. However, you can take even small steps to include the Designer of the Universe in lovemaking — for it is from that ocean of bliss that you share whenever you have sex. The key to discovery is to make love slowly. Begin with play, massage, and move into quiet stillness once you are joined. Remain motionless often, especially to control the male's excitement. During sex, practice measured breathing as you do during meditation. Circulate your energies, as described in the exercises below. Pray together during sexual union: Why not?

Abandoning his body at the gate of dreams the Spirit beholds, in awaking, his senses sleeping...in the region of dreams, wandering above and below the Spirit makes for himself innumerable subtle creations.

࿓ The Upanishads

Above all, feel sacred in the bosom of the universal creative forces and be grateful for the privilege of sexual expression.

Honor the sacredness of sex by enjoying sexual union as a rolling pattern of crests and valleys, rather than a singular explosion. The gentle Taoist techniques of physical love can be studied and learned to make specific use of the female's yin and the male's yang energies. However, there are exercises that you can practice, whether alone or with a partner, that can raise your awareness of these energies in your body.

Exercise 1 for Those without Partners: Sit comfortably on the floor, bed, or in a chair and follow the steps you normally follow for meditation. Once you are in a meditative or relaxed state, think about sex the last time you really enjoyed it. Breathe deeply — in through the nose and out through the open mouth. As your memory unfolds, allow yourself to feel aroused. Concentrate on the feelings in your heart, not just your physical sensations.

In order to discover your sexual *ch'i,* mentally isolate in your sexual organs the stirring of *ch'i* energy, visualizing it as an energy blooming just behind the physical. Concentrate on that nonphysical energy. Now, picture the energy as a sphere the size of a saucer, and picture it enlarging within you to the size of a dinner plate. Holding that thought, let the ball rise within you to the level of your heart. Try to draw the physical energy with it.

Practice sustaining this stimulation and visualization. Turn your thoughts away from the physical sex to the ideas of compassion and spiritual love. Now let the sexual *ch'i* charge your heart. Let the energy expand to encompass your whole body. Feel the energy lightening and stimulating, cleansing and purifying your organs, limbs, blood, and mind. As you breathe, picture the energy rising to the top of your head. In this state, express a prayer for some need that has been on your mind. Pray for the whole world, if you like. Finally, return the energy to its source without culminating a physical orgasm.

Practice this exercise until you discover the difference between physical stimulation and the *ch'i* energy that glows subtly behind it. Women will discover this more easily than men. Women should get comfortable identifying their energy as yin, and men as yang.

> God not only loves us in and through our sexuality but, of course, delights in our own human lovemaking. That love of beauty, union, and creativity is the sexual drive itself and God's gift. Sexuality is an aspect of our deeply human yearning for fulfillment and meaning, for God. In its total pervasion of our lives, Eros is the source of life and fuels all our loves — including our love for God!
>
> ∾ Dody H. Donnelly, *Radical Love*

A couple may use this exercise after each individual has practiced it. Practicing the exercise as individuals can prevent the excitement from overwhelming your perceptions of the subtle experiences taking place behind and above the physical.

Exercise 2 for Couples: Begin by facing each other in a seated position. Stimulation from memory should not be necessary, but partners should be sufficiently comfortable with each other so as not to feel embarrassed by nudity or sexual responses. At this time, as arousal turns on the sexual energy in your bodies, let each of you visualize the *ch'i* energy expanding within you. Raise it to the level of the heart, as in the exercise above. Look at your partner and feel True Love for that person open in your heart. Visualize the risen sexual energy as love energy and pass it to your lover's heart, through the space between you. Before you physically join, practice this visualization a few times. Take turns passing this energy and receiving it.

While still in a meditative state, join physically in some comfortable position. Move only often enough to keep the male stimulated. Visualize the yin and the yang energies flowing from each of your bodies at the point where your sexual organs have joined. You should be able to feel it flowing back and forth behind the physical pleasure of sexual joining. Take turns breathing the energy into and out of your bodies: The female draws the yang energy into her body on the inhale, pours yin energy into her partner on the exhale, and so forth. Exchange *ch'i* in this way for three or nine cycles. Then concentrate on your hearts.

When joined sexually, practice exchanging pure, clean, clear loving energy from heart to heart. Allow your sexual organs to disappear from the experience. Let your male and female energies, now shared equally within you, make you whole. Let the masculine and feminine blend into one. Include a few moments of prayer whenever you make love together — it all adds up to a more sacred experience of sex.

The energy work described in Exercise 2 is also helpful for couples who are separated by absences of time or distance. When

Just as sexual energy has helped man out of his spiritual state into the body, so it can help him to return in full awareness to his divine primal state of wholeness.

   ✐ Elizabeth Haich,
Sexual Energy and Yoga

you cannot be together, what better way to feel close than by spending some time communing in spirit with your partner? Set a time, meditate, use your sexual energy to send love across the miles — in terms of consciousness, distance does not exist. At the appointed hour, visualize your lover being encircled with this energy. Let the *ch'i* that you have raised now expand beyond your room and your house. Nothing is stopping you from surrounding the entire globe with this energy. Sending out your *ch'i* energy while you are apart helps the time pass.

The extent to which one can deepen the experience of sex can range from mild awareness to intense study, discipline, and practice — it is all up to you. These exercises are meant to help individuals and couples achieve a basic awareness of the hidden *ch'i* energy behind sex and to realize that your sacred sexuality is part of the created universe; part of the very creative energy of the Highest Power. Sexuality is a ray in the spectrum of light, which is consciousness itself. It is the mechanism by which human beings enjoy the very spark of life.

Flower Arrows

Who has never heard of the ancient *Kama Sutra of Vatsyayana,* the so-called "sex manual" of India? Few realize, however, that this work is actually a text rich in spiritual guidelines.

Western religions would be hard put to list only four basic components of human existence and the meaning of life. In India, however, a simple formula has been followed for thousands of years. For Hindus, the goals of human life are

- *Dharma:* Right living and right conduct

- *Artha:* Accumulation of material goods

- *Kama:* Desire, sensual pleasure, love

If these three are practiced satisfactorily in life, one will be entitled to

- *Moksha:* The liberation of the soul from the need to return to earth

In Hindu thought, *dharma* and *artha* are first in importance,

---

Bedtime Story

The coil spring was invented in Watertown, New York, by James Liddy in the 1850s.
He was leaning on a wagon one day, waiting to go home and tighten the ropes of his lattice bed, when he fell against the spring seat of his buggy. Once home he designed the coiled bedspring. By the 1930s, machine-made innerspring mattresses were installed on most beds.

Sacred space is a space
that is transparent to
transcendence, and
everything within such a
space furnishes a base for
meditation.... When you
enter through the door,
everything within that
space is symbolic,
the whole world
is mythologized.

∽ Joseph Campbell

although one has an obligation to succeed in all three. If *kama,* the need for sensual pleasure, is allowed to degenerate into a lifeless routine restricted to procreation, we tragically lose one of our greatest divine gifts and deny who we are — deny our Maker's imprint in our very being. Like other qualities of life, Hindus personify *kama* as the god Kama, who, Cupid-like, shoots flower arrows into the hearts of the unsuspecting, enflaming them with love. Kama's arrows are bound by neither caste, gender, nor age.

The famous *Kama Sutra* was never intended as a sex manual as we think of one in the West, but as a guide for people to succeed in *kama.* It was meant to keep sexuality alive and fun for couples, within the greater context of our spiritual makeup. It is as much a guide for morality and ethics as it is for more fully exploring the physical landscape of sexual pleasure.

Hindu sexual symbology shows none of the artificial politeness of Western society. It unapologetically represents the male and female principles with representations of the sexual organs: a lingam (phallus) and a yoni (vagina). The *Kama Sutra* urges partners to have pride, not shame, during sex, because joy in sex is a reflection of joy in union with the Divine.

Through *kama,* it is believed that one can attain both unity and reality. Incorporating one's sexuality into a regimen of worship, one can come to understand that unity and reality are one and the same. Our participation in *kama* links us with the primordial principle of desire out of which all creation came. *Kama* is the common element that underlies all things, the unifying principle — as the third part among *dharma* and *artha* — to which we return when we make love. This unifying force can be none other than a part of what we call God.

The symbolic art of Hinduism often shows its gods "in consort," or sexual union, with their counterpart goddesses. (See Figure 6.1.) But this is merely a metaphor for deeper realities on many levels. The male united with the female represents the masculine and feminine forces united into the totality of oneness. In Hinduism, the male and female aspect of the image of God is portrayed by the male Shiva and female Shakti.

Figure 6.1

In Buddhism, deities in consort symbolize the joining of opposite forces in the universe, for example, the principles of consciousness and energy; spirit and matter; the masculine and feminine principles. When in consort with your lover in the sacred bedroom, think of the divine principles that make up your inner identity.

Deities depicted in consort can represent balance within the individual, union between the soul and the Creator, as well as sexual union in all its divine characteristics: procreation, love, unity, ecstasy. Hinduism teaches that, later in life, one should overcome bodily attachments, including the desire for sex, in order to be truly free and spiritually accomplished. With this in mind, the image of the conjoined male and female deities represents not coition, but an individual who possesses the idealized qualities of both masculine and feminine, perfectly married to Spirit within.

In Hindu mythology, the symbolic powers of the male are exemplified in the figure of Shiva, the dancing god who makes the world go around. The goddess Shakti is the feminine, creative principle. The next time you make love, spend ten minutes in still silence. Contemplate how in your union duality dissolves. You become one as a tribute to the One True God. Seated together as Shiva and Shakti, embrace, meditate, and breathe deeply as you experience all duality dissolving into one. As an experiment, feel free to call each other by these names to help you discover the principles that otherwise hide behind your personalities.

Despite the lascivious reputation of the *Kama Sutra,* its practices were intended for married people to use. In India, even today, marriage is considered a sacred duty. Permanent celibacy, except for ascetics, is unacceptable. The *Kama Sutra* puts forth the important point that, while ignoring your sex life is harmful, indulging in lust is also harmful, interfering with living the *dharma.* "Kama

Tonight is a night
of union and the
scattering of the stars,
for a bride is coming
from the sky:
the full moon.
The sky is an astrolabe,
and the Law is Love.

∼ Rumi

cannot quench *kama*," it states. Without balance, sexual indulgence begets desire for more sexual indulgence. In a contradictory fashion, the sacred Hindu text *Bhagavad Gita* concurs, advising that *kama* is a source of pain as ignorance is a source of laziness. As it turns out, that is just the way the Buddha saw it.

Tantra Plays Peoria

Buddhists do not acknowledge the existence of a supreme deity, per se, existing apart from the totality of the All. In Buddhism, all is one, therefore all is sacred. Even though it does not acknowledge God, other than Buddhahood, Buddhism is a path to nirvana (heaven) through detachment from desire and compassion for all beings.

During Buddha's lifetime, sex was forbidden to followers who desired enlightenment, in the belief that, for most people, sex distracts the mind from inner calmness. In Zen Buddhism, the acquisition of true detachment allows a fuller engagement in sexuality while placing an importance upon it that is equal to crossing the street.

Around the middle of the first century C.E., Buddhism and Hinduism alike were influenced by the emergence of Tantrism, a philosophical approach whose roots predate the Vedas. Tantrism views sexuality as no more or less important than any other part of life.

When Tantric philosophy came West, it was often misrepresented and oversimplified as an exotic sexual science that everyone should try at home. Sexuality is of no more or less importance than, say, eating, working, or worshipping. However, there are many schools of Tantrism, and their practices range from no sexual activity at all to gross overindulgences.

Whether Hindu or Buddhist, the "right-hand" path of Tantrism maintains that sexual union should only be thought of as a symbolic union between the masculine and feminine principles that join together within the individual. The "left-hand" school maintains that sexual ritual is engaged in only after rigorous meditation, prayer, and visualization training, while avoiding orgasm completely. Sexual union is used in these instances as a way to reach nirvana, with neither lust, attachment, nor infatuation between

In the final analysis, our sexual malaise turns out to be a spiritual problem. We experience ourselves at odds with the universe at large, alienated from what theologians have called the ground of being. In many ways, we have lost sight of the sacred. Our lives are marked by an unhappy rift between the sacred and the profane.

⁓ Georg Feuerstein,
Sacred Sexuality

partners, who change from ritual to ritual. Sexual union is only used as a means to a heightened mental and spiritual experience.

In *The World's Religions: Our Great Wisdom Traditions*, theologian Huston Smith writes, "Tantra's teachings about sex are neither titillating nor bizarre: they are universal. Sex is so important — after all, it keeps life going — that it must be linked quite directly with God....Sex is the divine in its most available epiphany. But with this proviso: It is such when joined to love."

In authentic Tantric practice, sex is merely one aspect of the totality of life. Unifying the individual with that totality is Tantrism's goal. In recognizing the power of sexuality to degenerate into base, self-destructive behavior, authentic Tantrism emphasizes controlling desire and using sex for higher goals. Tantrism promotes the equality between men and women as partners. In the many branches that emphasize goddess worship, the woman, again, is elevated in importance during sexual ritual.

Most Westerners do not have the time or inclination to study the complexities of Tantrism; however, including some of its ideas in the sacred bedroom can be beneficial. Consider the yogi, who works toward enlightenment by practicing compassion and divesting him- or herself of attachments to the world. You can also learn from the Tantrist, who accomplishes this by including pleasure — not for the sake of pleasure, but for the higher conscious experience of blissful emptiness achieved by motionless meditation while in union with an enlightened partner. Let sex for you and your partner be an experience with the Divine. Save up your physical and emotional energies for it, as in a bank account. Make sexual encounters special in the knowledge that sex is an accepted, sanctified part of you. Attempt to glimpse what the Tantrists call the "mind of clear light."

Jeffrey Hopkins writes, in *Tibetan Arts of Love:* "During orgasm the subtlest and most powerful of all consciousnesses, the mind of clear light manifests, albeit only unconsciously to the untrained."

He states that the mind of clear light is what remains when all the lower minds have melted in bliss of intense orgasm. "The fundamental state — which dawns in conscious orgasm — is not a dimming of the mind, although it is often experienced as such

Bedtime Story

City apartments gave rise to the hideaway Murphy bed, which could be made to disappear into the living room wall. The unfolding sofa bed came on its heels.

Do we wish for our
beloved...is there aught
else for which we long,
yet for all our longing
do not obtain?
Lo, all shall be ours
if we but dive deep
within, even to the lotus
of the heart, where
dwells the Lord.

⮑ Chandogya Upanishad

because all of the usual conceptual minds are withdrawn during it. Rather, it is the basis of all phenomena. . . . " As the lower states of consciousness fall away, new conscious experiences emerge, leading lovers to being one with the sky and eventually to the mind of clear light.

These lofty states of consciousness are described in non-Tantric Buddhist and Hindu branches without inclusion of sexuality at all. They are provided here simply to stimulate your imagination to the possibilities as you explore sex in your sacred bedroom. The authentic Tantrist seeks to transform sexual energy into a transcendent force.

Like the Tantrist, you can exercise your sexual practices with periods of planned abstinence and purification rituals, followed by extended sessions that incorporate prayer in the form of chanting, meditation, and visualization. Live, sleep, and love together for a week, two weeks, or a month. Raise your sexual energy, bless it, turn it into selfless love, and look forward to a lovely night of lovemaking at the end of the abstinence, a week or a month away. Begin your celebration with a noontime meal. All day, look forward to your sacred bedroom encounter. Do something special together that day. Hold hands. Go out to dinner. Later, with your candles lit and your hearts open in True Love, you will become one together in what can be the most glorious of experiences in your sacred bedroom. Above all, experiment, and avoid making too much of a study of this glorious activity.

At lovemaking's best, when we are loved and in love, uncorrupted by artificial expectations, every fiber of our being is energized and in unabashed union with God. The power of arousal and the delightful sensations of the body send electrical energy throughout the nervous system. Time stops. Our breath and beating hearts, as we urgently love the beloved, become single-pointed. The mind, undistracted, leaves the ground of analysis and takes to the air. The soul expands beyond the body, becoming larger than the room, tasting at the edges of its expansion the flavors of the infinite. The higher consciousness of enlightened sex overlays the pattern of God-Is-Love, the heart's living guest.

FINDING YOURSELF IN THE OTHER

In the sacred bedroom, try to approach sex the same way you approach prayer and meditation. Think of your bed as a holy place, whether for repose, dreaming, contemplation, or sexual enjoyment. Expand your awareness of how sexuality reflects the image of God. And explore how you and your partner can achieve unity with the sacred when you make love.

Be sure to bear in mind that the purpose of seeking the sacred in sexuality is not to be pious while you are having sex, but to achieve a greater, lasting joy through the knowledge that your enjoyment of bliss is divinely ordained. The goal is to discover ways to have fun during sex while knowing that your lovemaking experiences are sacred. This is the crossroad where the black negligee and the Bible reside comfortably side by side with the lights on. It is where shame and guilt are left behind in the Dark Ages, where they belong.

As your sexual experiences grow in their spiritual qualities, you may wonder how to keep that glorious feeling all the time. However, one cannot have sex twenty-four hours a day, though young lovers sometimes try. The bonus is that you do not have to be having sex in order to maintain that mystical, above-the-body state of consciousness. Surely, you cannot, nor should you desire, to be physically stimulated all day. But the inner energy and exhilaration that you will come to know through the exercises separating the physical from the *ch'i* energy can give you a blissful attitude toward life.

Imagine what it would be like if your emotions, physical passion, mental intent, and actual practice could unite together, focused through the powerful lens of True Love. In True Love, your state of consciousness, if not the physical sensations, can accompany you throughout your day. It can sweeten all your relationships and help you stay in the never-ending moment of love, whatever you may be doing, because it banishes the ego to the background. Keeping mindful of this on a daily basis is not difficult. Strange as it may sound, your schoolroom for developing this

Spirit is everywhere,
upon the right,
upon the left, above,
below, behind, in front.
What is the world
but Spirit?

∽ The Upanishads

*Where the flesh is one,
one also is the spirit.
Together husband and
wife pray, together
perform their fasts,
mutually teaching,
exhorting, sustaining.
Equally they are found in
the church of God,
equally at the banquet
of God, equally in
persecutions and
in refreshments.*

ℂ *Tertullian,
To His Wife*

capacity is in the bedroom: if you are willing to try giving totally to your partner during sex.

Perhaps the most intriguing riddle of a sacred bedroom is how to give selflessly during the very act that brings to you the greatest pleasure. The fact is that the one can lead to the other. The key is your knowledge of the energy involved. It is the awareness of the hidden dynamics of a touch, an embrace, a kiss. It is a complete givingness followed by a disappearance of self, one into the other. True Love does not expect something in return. It is pure and simple giving. All is one.

True Love can be practiced in your caresses, kisses, and embraces so easily. Every touch becomes a symbol of True Love, played out in the realm of the senses and the body. When you make people feel good about themselves with some verbal comment, is it not an embrace on a higher level? When you help someone over a difficult problem, is it not a caress? When you open someone's heart with an expression of kindness, is it less than a tender kiss at some higher vibration? The effect is the same if you are feeling True Love in your heart. Despite its apparent power, sexuality is not the most powerful engine of divine creativity. The heart is the greater engine, because it transcends the limitations of the body and its nervous system.

In *The Knowing Heart: A Sufi Path of Transformation,* Kabir Helminski writes: "We have a heart, by which is meant an organ of perception through which the reality of Spirit can be apprehended. We cannot begin the spiritual journey unless the 'eye of the heart' is at least slightly open. It is for the heart to know that Reality which is not immediately apparent to the intellect or the senses. Every other organ of perception discerns through its own limited window; only the heart sees from all sides at once and can perceive Oneness." The effect of a loving act lives on in eternity, while a mere orgasm ends once the body is spent.

Finding your sacred self in the beloved is easy, once you get over the hurdle of expecting customized pleasures being exacted on your own body. The key is changing your attitude through elevated awareness of the hidden energies of sex. One way to discover it is in the following exercise: Have sex with your partner while ritualizing the steps. The purpose of this exercise is, as you become aware of the separate energies, to separate your selfish desires from expressions of True Love.

A True-Love Exercise

To explore True Love during sex, plan a sexual encounter for some evening when you will not be disturbed. Let every aspect of your encounter keep you mindful of its higher purpose.

In preparation for the encounter, purchase two white candles, the color symbolizing the pure spiritual energies that will be the carrying forces of your experience. Carefully choose your incense or essential oil. If you desire music, let it be quiet instrumental music, such as a flute or harp, or anything that will not distract. Silence may be preferable for concentration.

1. Begin with a ritual bath or shower. As you wash each other's body, concentrate on the symbolic washing away of expectations, fears, memories of past experiences, and anxieties. Wash away everything, except total love and dedication to your partner — to God-Is-Love disclosed within you. All your focus now is on feeling love.

2. Wear some special garments. For example, wear white silk robes, to help set this sexual experience off from routine sex. Use a special cloth or bedspread with a bright pattern or symbol to enhance the feeling of purpose. You may display a specially coordinated set of pillows to be used only during sacred sex.

Fresh from the washing ritual, dressed in your ceremonial clothes, sit before the altar facing each other.

3. Each of you light a candle for the other. Read or recite the following words:

Partner #1: "[Name], I light your flame in celebration of True Love, to share our creative energy together."

Partner #2: "[Name], I light your flame. May we commemorate the Father-Mother God and drink of the creative energy of our sexuality."

Now, facing each other, place your palms together and look

How it is I know now; but there is no place like a bed for confidential disclosures between friends. Man and wife, they say, there open the very bottom of their souls to each other; and some old couples often lie and chat over old times till nearly morning.

       ∽ Herman Melville, *Moby Dick*

The kingdom of God
is within you.

Luke 17:21

softly into each other's eyes. Meditate for a moment on allowing the truth in your hearts to speak to each other through your eyes. (Let one partner hold the paper that contains the prayers.)

Together: "The altar is now alight with flame, symbol of the Word, the Holy Logos of I AM that originally separated the dry land from the firmament."

4. Light the incense or essential oil burner. Partner #1 now lights the incense or essential oil burner as partner #2 reads:

The incense symbolizes Spirit that permeates all things. Spirit is eternal and can never be extinguished. We light the incense as a symbol of our souls uniting in body, mind, and spirit.

5. Make a special invocation to the Creative Force. Face each other again and place the palms of your hands together. Read or recite in unison:

Surround our lovemaking with pure white energy. Bless our bed and sacred bedroom space. Help us seek true love in our sexual communion with Thee. Let our sexual energy heal each other as we learn true giving. Help us retain True Love in our hearts every day.

You can incorporate as many prayers or variations as you wish, but it is important to dedicate your sexual experience to a higher purpose and invite Deity (God, Jesus Christ, Buddha, Elijah, the angel Gabriel, or another) to be present with you.

6. Lovemaking. Ring the bell and rise to your feet. For the lovemaking experience itself, try to keep a simple structure in mind:

- Greeting
- Warming
- Unity
- Gratitude

Greeting: Remove your clothing and stand at the foot of the bed. Each partner places his or her right hand over the heart of the other partner and repeats:

[Name], I stand before you naked in body, mind, and spirit. In the name of I AM THAT I AM, I dedicate God in Me to God in You in lovemaking as in life.

The greeting can be as simple as this, or you can elaborate, as with the rest of these suggestions, as you wish.

Warming: Now, situate yourselves on the cloth on the bed. Sit in the lotus position or some other position, facing each other. Let lovemaking begin with a slow kiss, and then progress naturally, however God-Is-Love guides you from within. Enjoy all the senses as they come into play. Go slowly. Take a full minute with each new action to allow warming to flood the body. Channel your energy upward and outward beyond your body and your room. Try to use restraint as passion builds. Remember to breathe deeply and slowly. Let the fire of sex energy cool, expand, and fill your body, not just tickle the sex organs. With each kiss, caress, and embrace, keep present in your mind the idea of your open heart — total love for the partner without restriction. Repeat the following with each action:

My prayer is to bring you to oneness with the Creator.

Try to bask in the spirit of that prayer for a few minutes before you lie down on the bed together.

Oneness: The male and female join their bodies. The mechanics of fulfilling, loving sex, including positions, timing, and techniques, can be as you wish. However, the point of this exercise is to give you time to explore the landscape of the Divine through selfless devotion to your holy partner. The time spent in that supercharged inner space, where normally you are concerned with either how your body feels or how much you love your partner, will give you invaluable experience in approaching "sky dancing."

In the height of pleasure, keep your mind focused on giving to your partner. The happy paradox of this approach to lovemaking is that as you attempt to give totally to the other, it is therefore part of your experience to enjoy what your lover is doing for you. By enjoying your partner's arts and sciences, you are giving yet again! The key is to realize that the more you give, the higher you can carry each other. In selfless True Love, your bodies can seem to disappear into each other. Your hearts open fully, and your tears

> Until now most human beings have remained quite ignorant of their own loving potential. We human beings are able to make love more frequently and sensuously than perhaps any other animal. Yet we are often disappointed after love-making. Why? Because most of us are like owners of a precious Stradivarius violin that we have never learned to play.
>
> ᗫ Jolan Chang, *The Tao of the Loving Couple*

A historical romance is the only kind of book where chastity really counts.

      ℃ Barbara Cartland

will flow as they did when you were children. Think of the yin-yang symbol as you give and receive during lovemaking, and all will become clear. (See Figure 6.2.)

As you make love, understand the energies of sex and circulate them to each other for healing. Be the respectful observer, aware that the greater experience of sex is not just physical but spiritual. The physical pleasure of sex is a tangible reflection of union with the Divine. Physical bodies become a cartoon of the union of the higher masculine and feminine principles, the uniting of matter and spirit. Let go of self, even the self that is trying to please. Enjoy the energy. Relish the physical ecstasy you achieve, and do not worry about orgasm. If it happens, let it happen. Men can study the techniques of semen retention and discover an entirely new world of sexuality. A man can learn the subtle power of a woman's body and her waves of pleasure. He may follow her, as the Taoists do, and love her all the more. If you each lose yourself in the other, you can catch a hint of the mystery of I AM THAT I AM.

The "True Love" Paradox

Partner A:
Total Giving

Partner B:
Total Giving

Figure 6.2

For partners giving totally during sex, receiving (R) is part of your partner's expectations for you.

When orgasm occurs, it can be a lightning bolt of creation or an ocean swell of liberation. Try to let orgasm arrive naturally, without using mental tricks or artificial imagery to bring it about. During orgasm, try to think strictly that your climax is a drop in the ocean of the Creator's love — for we know that to be true. When each of you perfects True Love in your heart, you will find yourself — your best Divine Self — living in your beloved's heart. God-Is-Love discovers God-Is-Love. I AM THAT I AM restates itself. Now you can live in the ecstasy of that awesome reality and live it throughout your day tomorrow.

Discovering True Love During Sex	
True Love is...	During sex, try to...
Patient	Be patient with irritating inconsequentials such as awkwardness. Be patient with orgasm, for yourself and your lover. Be patient even if orgasm does not come.
Kind	Think of lovemaking as a high-society dinner: Always use your best manners, and try to anticipate ways in which you can make your partner comfortable. Hold your partner's head; slip a pillow in just the right spot. Use gentle touch. Test things you want to try, slowly.
Forgiving	Forgive all errors, clumsiness, the pushing of negative emotional buttons, and even your pet turn-offs. It is our humanness that we are leaving behind, our sacred divine nature that we are honoring.
A mystical marriage	Remember that the two of you together marry the masculine and feminine. With True Love in your heart, you are also marrying God within. Be mindful during sex how close to the sacred you are.
God within you	Recognize that, like you, your partner is trying to manifest God-Is-Love. Keep in mind that the image of God is within you, even and especially, during sex.
Beyond romance	See beyond your romantic fervor, visualizing your partner as a stranger in the street you have never seen before. See your partner as others see him or her, and let True Love continue to love them.
Beyond change	Picture your lover in his or her eighties, wrinkled and old, even infirm, but let True Love continue to bloom. Picture your lover changed in a variety of ways you would not wish, and practice love unchanged. This is True Love.

He who gives himself to vanity, and does not give himself to meditation, forgetting the real aim [of life] and grasping at pleasure, will in time envy him who has exerted himself in meditation.

∽ **The Dhammapada**

Gratitude: After your structured sexual celebrations, be sure to offer gratitude in as grand a production as you can. Express gratitude to your Creator who provided you with sex for expressing love and procreating humankind. Also, be sure to express gratitude to your partner.

> *Together:* "We thank the Creator by whose gift of love we experience the joy of creation with our bodies. We are grateful to each other for sharing the miracle of oneness in body, mind, and spirit."

An added value of the sexual exercise above is how it affects your thinking the next day. Sacred sex has been known to keep participants smiling irresistibly around the clock. Higher-consciousness sex can help you see otherwise hidden spiritual realities when sex is enjoyed by two partners deliberately focusing on love. With both partners giving totally, the receiving increases a thousandfold. Kindnesses spill over to and from the individual after some practice. The resulting energy is abundant for getting through your day of work and play.

It is so much easier to express love in wise measures throughout the day, after having expressed it during an ordinarily selfish act (sex) that delivers the greatest pleasure to the individual. This is a secret for overcoming sexual preoccupations. A secret to overcoming low self-esteem. A secret to understanding what God-Is-Love means in the day-to-day rat race — only the energy and putting love into action matter. The rest is minor in the light of True Love and its infinite blessings.

Spiritualizing the approach to sex in your sacred bedroom — even if intercourse is impossible or incomplete — can create wonderful, sacred experiences for partners who are willing to try. Praying together in bed, while embracing or giving a massage, can open the doors to intimacy in ways that can be very healing.

Many men and women mistakenly believe that if they experience their sexual energy, they must do something about it — they must perform, act it out, discharge it. Since having sexual energy is simply a function of being alive, all they need to do with it is experience it. They can learn to contain it and to allow it to spread out to the whole body rather than to express it genitally.

ꙮ Jack Lee Rosenberg,
Body, Self, and Soul

NOTES FOR SINGLES

People who live without partners can also benefit from enlightened sexuality. Some single people are happy without partners, while others long for a partner and suffer in their loneliness.

Knowledge of enlightened sexuality can relieve much of that suffering. Single people, too, when sexually aroused, can enter meditation. They, too, can be the observer of their sex energy and visualize that energy circulating in their bodies as healing energy. They can meditate on their own masculine and feminine nature within. They can raise that energy to the heart and use it as fuel for True Love: for their higher, sacred self and to nurture God within. They can consume their sex energy on the altar of the heart as fuel for sharing lovingness and being loving with people. Singles who do this make themselves more attractive to others. True Love conquers all. True Love is the most attractive quality one can adopt.

In *Passions of Innocence,* psychologist Stuart Sovatsky, Ph.D., explains the concept of Tantric celibacy and the yogic practice of refining sexual energy into creative resources through *brahmacharya* ("brah-mah-char-yah"). He teaches to teenagers this Indian concept, by which sexual energy is transformed into energy for meditation. Pent-up sexual energy can be transformed, by anyone, through breathing exercises and yoga. He suggests that sexual energy be "saved up" like cash. Individuals can then "spend" it in sex or in *brahmacharya*. The practice is excellent for single people of all ages who worry about sex or who feel frustrated.

"Given some months of practice," Sovatsky writes, "you might find that you like what *brahmacharya* enables you to buy: a sense of vibrancy, a closeness with others, an inspired creativity." Meditation disperses sexual energy, allowing it to rise up the spine and spread throughout the body. The practices of yoga and yogic breathing exercises are very helpful, whether you are celibate or sexually active.

Even if you have a partner, sometimes you will be apart. Awareness of sacred sex reveals that sexuality does not even require physical contact. Partners who have discovered the energies of sex learn that they can feel sensual and raise the flame of love when they think of each other. When you are apart, set a time each day when you can commune in your thoughts and heart. Amazing "coincidences" of communication can occur during these intimate at-distance sessions of communing with the one you love.

Empty yourself of
everything.
Let the mind rest
at peace.
The ten thousand things
rise and fall while the Self
watches their return.
They grow and flourish
and then return
to the source.
Returning to the source
is stillness,
which is the way of
nature.

    Tao Te Ching

Touch ultimate emptiness;
Hold steady and still.

∽ Lao-tzu

Recipes for the Sacred Bedroom

Due to their zinc content, oysters have been known since Roman times to increase sexual energy. For nonoyster eaters, try dates stuffed with almonds or make your favorite cookie recipe using ground pecans, Brazil nuts, honey, oats, and whole wheat.

7

The Sacred Bedroom Experience

Your sacred space is where
you find yourself again and again.

— Joseph Campbell

The sacred bedroom can become an important new setting for your spiritual practice. This potential bears new opportunities for personal growth as well as providing an intimate venue for overcoming challenges. A sacred bedroom can soften resistive partners and also provide personal sanctuary spaces for children.

A SACRED BEDROOM SCENARIO

The greatest gift of the sacred bedroom is helping you hold on to your connection with the Divine during that daily intermezzo between when you rise from bed and return to it at day's end. Your sanctuary makes this possible because you have increased your spiritual practice, the time you spend contemplating the Divine, during a greater portion of your day than ever before. The following narrative traces an evening in the life of David and Karen Maxwell, a couple whose sacred bedroom enhances their health and spirituality in every aspect of their lives.

Karen Maxwell arrives home from work at six o'clock. On her way into the living room, she sorts through the mail and then checks the answering machine. She sits facing the picture window and breathes a sigh of relief. Looking out at the woods beyond her yard, she draws in a deep breath and mentally reviews the events of her day. She argued with her secretary, only later realizing that she had been in the wrong. She apologized, but the mistake set her on edge for the rest of the afternoon. Not wanting to carry the residue of negative emotions into her sacred bedroom, Karen meditates for a moment to clear her mind. On a nearby pad of paper she makes notes for the following day, so she doesn't have to think about work again until morning.

Peeking into their rooms, she greets her two children, Will, eleven, and Katie, eight. He is listening to his stereo and she is browsing the Internet for a school assignment. Karen goes to the bedroom — the sacred bedroom that she and her husband turned into their personal sanctuary a year ago. With her right hand, she touches a white crystal star in the center of the door. This is the Maxwells' chosen symbol for the light of universal understanding.

Karen utters a prayer that she memorized for entering the sacred bedroom: "I leave negative thoughts and memories outside my sacred bedroom. May the light reconnect me to Spirit, restore my vitality, and open my heart."

Karen opens the bedroom door, revealing a bright, neatly decorated room of rich woods and green fabric walls. The afternoon sunshine is sweeping through white cotton draperies and across the bedclothes, also in white. The warm wood grain of the floor glows golden in the sunlight. On the wall over the bed hangs an image of the sun, symbol for I AM THAT I AM consciousness, and for the love Karen and David had pledged to each other on their wedding day.

Two small but comfortable meditation chairs sit across from their altar, set up on a narrow wooden table. The altar cloth is white, gold, and blue. A crystal sun symbol stands in the center,

The dream is a little hidden door in the innermost and most secret recesses of the psyche.

⁓ Carl Jung

flanked by figures of Christ and Mother Mary, a symbol, for them, of the mother aspect of God. On the right, they have placed a photo collage of their family in a gold frame. On the left is a framed photo of the earth green and brown, hanging in space in its blue mantle of the atmosphere. An incense burner, an essential oil burner, a crystal bell, a small Bible opened to a favorite passage, and an amethyst crystal cluster are in the center. A small statue of Buddha stands off to the side — a meditative image symbolizing mental and emotional control.

Karen slips off her clothes and puts them away, then pulls on a floor-length, woven cotton robe. She kneels before her altar, rings the crystal bell, and whispers a prayer of thanks for the day and for all she enjoys in life — her husband, children, home, and work.

"Bless my household, Lord. Keep True Love forever alive in our hearts."

Despite the stresses of the day Karen feels good. She doesn't have to wait until church on Sunday to feel in the Spirit. She feels refreshed and ready for the real life she lives with her family for the evening. She stands and goes to the kitchen to make dinner.

David comes home at seven. After looking in on the children and hugging Karen, he, too, takes a moment to unwind in the living room before entering the bedroom sanctuary space. His day was less stressful than Karen's. It had been pretty good, he thought. He had solved a major software problem at work and received news of a raise in pay that they had been hoping for. Even with his good news, David wants to enter the sacred bedroom centered and feeling free from the emotional tension of the day.

After a moment, David heads to the bedroom. The sun, red-orange now, illuminates the room, making it appear like an ancient temple. As he changes into comfortable clothes, he admires a small Tibetan tapestry on the wall opposite a wooden flute that was placed there to cure the feng shui. Ringing the crystal bell, he gives thanks for the day and goes out to the kitchen to help Karen finish dinner.

The children light the candles on the dinner table, and the family dines. They discuss the events of the day, reflecting on

> Thank God for sleep!
> And, when you
> cannot sleep,
> Still thank Him
> that you live
> To lie awake.
>
> ∽ John Oxenham,
> *The Sacrament of Sleep*

the positive and the negative things that occurred. They talk about a trip to the lake that they have been planning for the weekend. After they eat, they clean up the kitchen together, washing and drying the dishes. The Maxwells then watch a couple of television programs together, and retire for the evening.

With the children in their rooms for the night, David and Karen take each other's hands and close their sacred bedroom door behind them. In each other's eyes, they can see their history together.

The Maxwells had been married for twelve years, when, a year ago, things started getting edgy between them. Pressures of the job and demands of their children were only part of the story. Lovemaking had dwindled to about once per month, and, due to stress, had turned into an often hurried, distracted activity. On both of their minds had been a serious debt problem stemming from an investment gone bad. Full of blame, David and Karen were being rude to each other, occasionally snapping at one other over dinner, but especially when they were alone, in their bedroom, before sleep. They watched late-night TV, only turning it off when falling asleep.

The Maxwells did not want to use a marriage counselor — they had neither the time nor the money. Instead, they created a sacred bedroom. They let their sacred bedroom be the setting for an intensified spiritual practice as they healed. They agreed that whenever they entered the bedroom, they would leave their disagreements, concerns, and preoccupations at the door. They talked through their problems before entering the sanctuary. They knelt before their candlelit altar, their Bible open to a different passage every night, and asked Spirit to be their marriage counselor. They worked at True Love and found forgiveness. Soon they were back on track.

Just as they have been doing for the past year, David and Karen have a heart-to-heart talk before bed. They light candles and meditate together for five minutes. Having little practice in meditation, they simply try to keep their thoughts focused on love and free from worldly cares. They are now comfortable with that warming place of peace they find in meditation. Now, they light

God cannot catch us unless we stay in the unconscious room of our hearts.

ᖇ Patrick Kavanagh

candles and ring the bell to signal the end of their meditation. David reads aloud a passage from the Song of Songs.

They stand before their altar, embrace, and kiss. They let their clothes slide to the floor and admire each other in the candlelight. Recalling the divine image in the symbol of the mystical bride and groom, they invite God-Is-Love to inspire them to discover each other anew during lovemaking. They lie together on their bed and focus on the energy created by their being together. They make love and soon fall asleep in the bosom of their sacred bedroom for the night. In the morning, they each write down their dreams for discussion at breakfast or later in the day.

In the morning light, they exercise and shower, before joining each other for morning meditation. They emerge from their sacred bedroom refreshed physically, mentally, sexually, and spiritually. The kids go off to school, and David and Karen kiss once again before they head off to work, bearing in their hearts the precious gift of peace, cultivated in the sacred bedroom, which will remain with them throughout the day until they join for dinner.

Like the Maxwells, we can transform our lives through a conscientious spiritual practice. The bedroom space, with its redefined purpose, provides the setting for healing, nurturing, worship, and peace. Let the bedroom become a peaceful haven in the home that operates at the levels of the body, mind, and heart. Let it be a temple in which the powers of love and sex can invigorate you and your partner and energize the entire home.

> One has to be in the same place every day, watch the dawn from the same house, hear the same birds awake each morning, to realize how inexhaustively rich and different is sameness.
>
> — Chuang-tzu

MAKING IT WORK

A story is told in the Islamic tradition about a Shah Kirmani who did not sleep for forty years, but stayed awake praying and demonstrating his great religious zeal. Eventually, however, his eyes closed, his head nodded, and he was overwhelmed by sleep. Once asleep, he went into a dream and saw God.

"Oh Lord," he explained, "I was seeking Thee in nightly vigils, but I have found Thee in sleep."

"Oh Shah," answered God. "You have found me by means of

those nightly vigils: if you had not sought me there, you would not have found me here."

The point of the story is that seeking the sacred, in itself, brings us closer to the Divine in ways we may not plan or anticipate. Success in our spiritual life is not necessarily reaching some particular goal, but exists in the ongoing effort, practice, and intent to focus our minds and open our hearts on a daily basis. The great benefit is in the journey, perhaps more than the destination.

The key to succeeding with your sacred bedroom is willingness and making an effort to practice new habits. Spiritual nourishment is now built into your personal base of operations — the bedroom. Excuses for neglecting your spiritual life — indeed, separating your spiritual life from any other part of your life — have vanished. No longer can you say, "I don't have time to attend services" or "It's too hard to make myself sit down and meditate or pray."

It is well known that when you change your surroundings, you can change who you are. Consider the changes you may have already made. You have rearranged your bedroom space according to the principles of feng shui: new furnishings and a balanced flow of *ch'i*. You have incorporated holistic objects and materials into the room's plan, and eliminated disruptive influences, such as stereos, computers, and TVs. In their place, you have created an altar that holds symbols and images that make you feel closer to the sacred and remind you of the new purpose of your bedroom.

If you are maintaining a regular meditation practice, you can now take advantage of the bedroom's privacy and solitude to still the mind and arrest the effects of stress from the day. Whether in meditation, prayer, or contemplation, while seated before your altar, you can talk to the Highest Power and listen for answers as you enjoy in silence the counsel of your heart. In meditation, you practice tuning out the senses and stilling the mind for communication with the Divine. You are also aware of the ways to utilize the senses when enjoying the pure sensations of natural experience: aromatherapy, music, art, décor, and light.

Now, in your bed at night before you go to sleep, whether

There is only one time
when it is essential
to awaken.
That time is now.

～ Buddha

alone or with your lover, you can freely contemplate the image of God, I AM THAT I AM, the very engine of consciousness itself. You enter sleep with sacred purposes: for deep rest and recharging for health, but also for dreams, those messages from your Higher Self or even the Creator, by which you can gain guidance for your life. You spend fully one-third of your life slipping into and out of the dream world, where the dreaming mind experiences vast worlds of symbols and instruction. To the mind, the dream world is just as real as the waking world. That is why it is called the "dream life."

All these activities, when enjoyed in the spirit of True Love, brighten the colors of the personality and raise your awareness in the direction of God consciousness. All that is well and good. But circumstances sometimes interfere with the best of idealistic intentions: an uncooperative spouse; children barging in; travel; the uncertainties of dating. Here are some suggestions for solving some of these problems.

Resistive Partners

Creating a sacred bedroom in a house in which one spouse is opposed or indifferent to the idea is similar to any situation in which partners have differing beliefs. The main difference is that your bedroom space is as personal to that other person as it is to you. If you want to decorate the room, set up an altar, meditate, pray, or explore sacred sexuality, you must enlist the cooperation of your partner.

If your partner does not immediately take to the sacred bedroom idea, discuss the basis for the disagreement. Your partner may be of a different religious background or not be inclined to adopt a spiritual life at all. In either case, you may need to find your common ground and build a sacred bedroom space from there. The following steps may help in this undertaking:

1. **Find mutual areas of agreement.** If there are religious differences, find common ground in symbols for things you agree on. If your partner is willing to display a symbol of his or her own, perhaps you will be granted one of yours. Compromise. Work together to discover universal symbols

> Creation was for the purpose of lovemaking. As long as there was only one-ness, there was no delight. But when division occurred and afterwards they [man and woman] were connected with one another, this brought about great delight.
>
> ∽ Reb Hayim Haikel

for basic principles (light, love, et cetera) and display those. If possible, construct prayers and rituals in which these principles can be mutually honored.

2. **Consider creating a nonreligious altar.** Explain how we all make altars in our homes, arranged on the desk at work, placed on a mantle or piano or in display cases. Consider an altar of family photos. Explain how life is filled with little rituals, from reading the newspaper in the morning to watching TV at night. Explain the sacred bedroom in these terms so it does not seem so foreign.

3. **If you cannot find a common spiritual ground, then consider settling for physical improvements to the room.** Using feng shui, for example, is just part of redecorating. There is no need to convince your partner of the principles of feng shui or *ch'i*, et cetera, because you will both reap the benefits of feng shui whether one partner appreciates it or not. Decorating with a holistic view simply makes sense for good health.

4. **Set an example.** Keep a dream journal, meditate — maybe the other will become curious. Try not to flaunt your practices or dominate your partner with your ideas.

The possibility of increased sexual pleasure can be enough to persuade some partners to try sacred sexuality. If your partner will not budge, however, you can keep sex sacred in your own experience of lovemaking. Let the experience be what you wish it to be. Work with your energy. Make sacred your experience by recalling the many levels on which sex is connected to the Creator. Grow with sexuality, and try to see above the clouds through extended ecstasy, however you can find it. Try not to allow yourself to drift into resentment. If incompatibilities are severe, it may be that they are prevalent in other aspects of your relationship, and that general remedies, such as counseling, are in order.

You can enjoy the benefits of a sacred bedroom while still

> A man is shown in his dreams what he thinks in his heart.
>
> ∼ The Talmud

respecting the space of your partner. Depending on the willingness of your partner to cooperate, you may be able to do as you please while the partner merely tolerates it. You may need to confine your display items (sacred symbols, altar, et cetera) to one small corner of the room. The most important point is that even a small display serves as that daily reminder of the sacredness of your own soul, your connection to the Creator, the value of your dreams, and the privacy in which you return to your authentic self.

A New Partner

Many of the same steps apply for a new partner. If you are single and have set up a sacred bedroom for yourself, how do you introduce your lover to this concept? Aside from asking him or her to read this book, let trust be your guide. Until the time is right, keep your sacred bedroom private and off limits — as you would with the most personal information about yourself. After all, the bedroom space is your sacred ground. Treat the space with special reverence, because it is the place you have chosen to use for communing with the Divine in your prayers and meditations. When the time is right, share your sacred bedroom with a trusted date, partner, or even a friend. Merely let them know that, to you, this space is your personal sanctuary. It is free of rancor, conflict, and harsh words or feelings of any kind. The space and energy of your sacred bedroom are hallowed.

Let the words
of my mouth, and the
meditation of my heart,
be acceptable in thy sight.

ᴇ Psalm 19:14

Tips for New Bedroom Partners

- Protect your sacred sanctuary until your new partner proves worthy.
- Use other rooms for socializing and sexuality until you are comfortable sharing your sacred bedroom.
- Introduce your new partner to your sacred bedroom on the basis of trust and intimacy.
- Discuss your religious views, and establish your common ground of faith.
- Welcome your new partner after he or she knows how important your sacred bedroom is to you.

Children

If you have children in the house, help them to understand what it means to have a personal sanctuary. Depending on their age and sensibilities, their reactions may range from interest to indifference. If they are indifferent or opposed to the idea of your sacred bedroom, help them respect your need for this private space by explaining what it means to you.

Children, too, can benefit from keeping a sacred bedroom. However you teach your children in the ways of religious faith, the value of a sacred space for a child can be immeasurable. Try to communicate the importance of taking time apart from distractions to reflect in silence, especially if your child has a TV, computer, or stereo in the room. Help children choose some corner of the room where they can display symbols of their faith as reminders that, even when life gets rough, they can turn off all the distractions and emotionally and mentally center themselves, pray, meditate, and listen for answers to problems.

> Sleep is
> the best meditation.
>
> ∾ The Dalai Lama

A Sacred Bedroom for a Child

Instruct your children in the importance of respecting your personal sanctuary. Help them discover what is sacred to them and

1. Understand the importance of spending quiet time in contemplation
2. Choose sacred objects and images
3. Set aside a table or corner of their room for an altar
4. Record and interpret their dreams
5. Understand their connection to the Divine

Suggest an altar for your child from the child's point of view. For infants, you can create a small altar on a shelf over the crib, keeping it out of reach. For older children, make suggestions, such as a symbol of the Divine Mother (e.g., Mother Mary or Kuan Yin), other religious symbols according to your faith, and items from nature, such as dried flowers, crystals, or shells. Also suggest a photo collage — which may include photos of Mom and Dad, grandparents, siblings, or others.

Children are naturally open to their dream life and often find it easier than adults to find meaning in them. Guide them in the process described in chapter 4 for titling and recording their dreams. Use your best judgment regarding incense in their rooms, as young children should not have access to matches or essential oils.

Above all, help children realize that they can be happier in their stressful lives by following some of these procedures. Let children know that their sacred space and altar connect them to the Allness, the Creator, to God the Father and God the Mother, according to their beliefs. They can make their bedroom more personal and private, in that way.

Travel

When you are traveling you can take with you a small, portable altar or simply an object or two from your home altar. In this way, you can bring reminders of your sacred space even to a hotel room — really just another bedroom. Whether you stay in a ship's cabin, train sleeper, even a sleeping bag under the stars, a candle, religious symbol, altar cloth, bell, or crystal from your altar can help keep you mindful of Spirit. If bringing something along is not possible or convenient, a simple prayer will suffice to put you in a sacred frame of mind at bedtime.

In considering how to make the sacred bedroom work best for you, remember to simplify, rather than further complicate, your life. In other words, incorporate these ideas one step at a time, or, if you wish, use them selectively, in cooperation with the other members of your household. Solve challenges creatively as you work toward including everyone in your discoveries of the sacred in your everyday life.

> Of so many teachers I've met in India and Asia, if you were to bring them to America, get them a house, two cars, a spouse, three kids, a job, insurance, and taxes...they would all have a hard time.
>
> ⚭ Pir Vilayat Khan

EXPANDING THE DREAM

The spirituality you practice in your sacred bedroom need not be a prisoner of the bedroom space. It can be expanded to enhance your "other life" — the one you live out there in the world.

Bedtime Story

The waterbed came
into popularity
during the 1970s,
but did not last long.
It is said that waterbeds
interfere with proper
feng shui in the bedroom.

∽

In the bedroom, as in no other place, your most honest personal thoughts and feelings rise to the surface. Through a regular spiritual practice of meditation, prayer, contemplation, and sacred lovemaking, you can light the flame of spiritual awareness and keep that flame burning brightly in every arena of your life.

If you keep your sacred bedroom feelings alive in your heart, you can always dwell in that inner peace that you visit when you are in your personal sanctuary. The more time you spend living life as the authentic you, the more at peace you can be outside the bedroom and outside the home.

The world makes it difficult to maintain your spiritual equilibrium, as people, circumstances, and media chip away at it. These influences draw out particular desires and emotions that prod the ego to dominate the heart. The sacred bedroom space affords you the private environment in which to heal from the daily assault of the materialistic world and helps you spend more time enjoying your spiritual life for peace of mind, increased self-esteem, personal growth, and guidance from within. You are, in effect, mending the division between church and state in your psyche. With this new attitude, you can bless all the natural aspects of your life in the light of spiritual truth.

If you are like me, your spiritual practice is far from perfect. It is sometimes difficult not to be in a rush. We cannot practice all of the sacred bedroom activities every day. For example, it's all too easy to put off meditation. However, there are five basic principles from *The Sacred Bedroom* that can help you maintain your spiritual ideals: the divine image within, True Love, energy, filtering the artificial, and honoring your authentic self. Type them onto a business-size card and keep it in your wallet. (See the "Sacred Bedroom Principles Card" on page 165.)

The divine image within: Remember that you are not just your body. You are a dynamo of consciousness, an eternal soul temporarily inhabiting a body that was made in the image of God. However you conceive of the Creator of All That Is, you can feel your direct connection to that awesome power in your I AM THAT I AM consciousness. Be aware of the masculine-feminine forces that you blend within you and with your partner. Remember this while driving to work, throughout your day of interactions with bosses, coworkers, subordinates. Each person you meet is connected at these levels to the Divine within. Remember also that God-Is-Love resides within your heart and that you can open the floodgates of love at any time you wish.

Sacred Bedroom Principles Card

Write these principles on a card to post on your altar or tuck into the frame of a bedroom mirror to help you maintain your perspective:

The divine image within
True Love
Energy
Filter the artificial
Honor your authentic self

True Love: Think of the sacred bedroom as a laboratory for love that allows you to explore, express, and expand every sort of love because you are away from prying eyes and listening ears. Love of self, partner, family, and friends can be included in your meditations and visualizations. Best of all, you can know the love of the Creator because you have integrated into your spiritual life the previously secret side of your thoughts, feelings, and your very sexuality.

True Love is that sustaining spiritual love that goes beyond infatuation: love that transcends the changes in life and withstands the passage of time. True Love is God within You recognizing God within You in the other. It elevates the energy of sex from the body to a celebration of the soul. It takes the state of higher consciousness you achieve during sex and filters it into the rest of your life. It is about becoming one with God in this most natural of activities. True Love during sex is finding *yourself* — your best self — in the other. Remember also that every aspect of your happiness, self-esteem, and security is up to you and your attitude.

Energy: Wherever you go, be mindful of the energy in your body, around you, and in others. *Ch'i* flows through city streets,

God is love;
and he who dwells in
love dwells in God.

 ∽ I John 4:16

We can't help being thirsty moving toward the voice of water. Milk-drinkers draw close to the mother; Muslims, Christians, Jews, Buddhists, Hindus, shamans, everyone hears the intelligent sound and moves, with thirst, to meet it.

       Rumi

down country roads, around houses and buildings, in through doors and out through windows. It flows in your body. Keep your own *ch'i* high from your practices in meditation and sacred love-making: It will help you look and feel younger, give you more energy. See the ebb and flow of energy in others and realize that you can rise above the negativity in others and see clear to say or do just the right thing to make a situation better. Make up your mind to stop taking the words and actions of others personally, by perceiving the energy behind them.

You release energy whenever you speak or think a thought about others. Keep the heart engaged and love flowing, and you will realize that many problems are illusions and not problems at all.

Filtering the artificial: Whenever you watch TV, films, and videos, read newspapers and magazines, or surf the Internet, be aware that the intention of most media messages is commercial. Remember that persuaders are designed to stimulate your sexual and sensual desires or provoke emotional responses in order to break down your resistance to buy or buy into products or ideas. Try to keep your filter operating so the synthetic world around you neither carries you away from your spiritual centeredness nor artificially stimulates hungers within you that make you feel badly about yourself.

Honoring your authentic self: Your authentic self is the enthusiastic, questioning, cheerful child within that knows his or her place in the universe. It is the confident *you* that knows the permanence of the soul thriving behind the scene, no matter what you do. It is the *you* that first wakes in the morning and that at last slips back into sleep at night when the concerns of the world have lifted and you relax.

The above principles describe some of the elements belonging to any well-grounded spiritual practice. With the right bedroom attitude, you can keep yourself in the light of spiritual awareness, and then use what you practice there to thrive in modern life. In your bedroom, you can use ritual to reinforce your beliefs.

The rituals and celebrations described in chapters 5 and 6 were designed to help couples honor their relationships in romance and sexuality. However, there are many more rituals that you can use in the sacred bedroom to help establish new habits and a positive attitude.

The following rituals and celebrations can be used by anyone, with or without a partner, to practice communing with the sacred in exotic and interesting ways. Some of these rituals can be just for fun, but most can help you deepen your experience of the Divine in the sacred bedroom.

Schedule regular rituals in which you honor the Divine within you. If you share your bedroom with a partner, you can modify the rituals to include that partner by sharing the activities and prayers. For example, let one partner light the candles and ring the bell while the other reads the prayer. You may also read prayers in unison. Then take turns leading the rituals.

Entering the bedroom: Adopt a simple ritual for entering or leaving the bedroom in order to formalize your higher purpose for entering there. Begin by touching or otherwise honoring the small sacred symbol you placed on your door frame (see chapter 2) every time you enter or leave the bedroom. In this way you acknowledge that this is the sacred space in which you live one-third of your life. Whenever you enter the bedroom, even if you merely forgot something and had to return, use a simple prayer or affirmation such as

I enter this sanctuary for healing and peace. I shall bring no disharmony here.

If you have little privacy in your house, touching alone, along with a mental prayer or affirmation, will suffice. Once your practice becomes habitual, keep the meaning fresh by making changes in the routine or the words you use. Think of entering the portal of the bedroom as the transition from the chaotic outer world to the peace of your sanctified space.

Consecrating objects: Each time you add a new object to the altar or elsewhere in the sacred bedroom, celebrate and consecrate that item. For example, when you purchase new linens, why not light a candle and claim them as part of your experience in the sacred bedroom?

> Thou art Divine, I know,
> O Lord Supreme,
> Since God found
> entrance to my heart
> through Love.
> This taught me that
> for steady inner growth
> Quick and silent
> meditation is best.
>
> ∽ Zend-Avesta

I consecrate this [linen, candle, et cetera] to be part of the sacred purpose of my bedroom.

Adapt the affirmation above for use with all new objects, such as art, photographs, statuary, anything at all that brings honor to the sacred bedroom.

Meditating: Meditation and prayer are the "please and thank you" of our communication with the Creative Force. Prayer is asking and offering, while meditation is listening for the answers. Meditation helps you discover a quiet space within you that you can cultivate with practice and visit whenever you need to truly rest your mind, recharge your energy, or touch base with your genuine self. From that still point within your consciousness, you can more wisely judge what is going on around you and what to do about it.

Create simple ritual practices to honor the sacred event of meditation. Since meditation is the act of placing yourself in the presence of the Divine, each time you meditate, allow your heart to sing. Open your meditations with a reading or affirmation. Use a simple candle flame and a bell tone to acknowledge the beginning and end of a meditation session.

At the close of meditation, express your gratitude for this time and place apart from the hassles of the world with another affirmation or expression of how you feel. I use the Lord's Prayer. I also use *om mani padme hum* ("hail to the jewel in the lotus"), which, to me, expresses our oneness with God-Is-Love, with all our brothers and sisters, and all of life. I use this because this is what I strive to feel whenever I meditate. But you can use whatever you wish — whatever connects you to what is sacred to you. Officially close your meditation session by ringing the bell and extinguishing the candle.

With practice, the peaceful center you achieve during meditation can accompany you throughout the day, or at least stay within reach with brief meditations during the day. While you are at work, take time in your office, outside, or even in the washroom, if necessary, to keep "in touch" with your authentic self, the one you practice in the bedroom. If possible, keep some small reminder of what you hold sacred on your desk or near your work space. The benefit is that regular meditation can reduce stress and its effects on your mind and body.

To give pleasure
to a single heart
by a single act is better
than a thousand heads
bowing in prayer.

Mahatma Gandhi

Praying: People the world over pray in many different ways. Unless your beliefs specify some singular practice, you can explore these rich traditions of prayer. The idea is to find for yourself a practice that keeps the spirit of prayer fresh and genuine. The simplest act of prayer, if it constitutes repetition of words or is framed within a set of customs, is already ritualized. You can establish a prayer ritual for yourself that is brief or lengthy, depending upon your purpose. You can repeat prewritten prayers, as is done with the Catholic rosary, in Buddhist chanting, and in many other religions. However, remember to include a moment in which you talk to God the way you would talk to a trusted friend — just use words that express what is in your heart.

Guiding dreams: Remember that you can incubate dreams about any aspect of your life, and this includes your work and social arenas. Dreams depict your life translated back to you in symbols and analogies. While they are sometimes generated by physical conditions, weighty concerns, or unobserved situations, they also can convey genuine inspiration from your Higher Self (your soul) or from the mind of the Creator.

Therefore, if you are trying to assess a potential new partner, or find insight into problems with a spouse, child, or relative, a dream can often point the way to solving the problem — if nothing else, dreams can reveal the part of the problem that you contribute! The same is true for a difficult situation on the job, for example, with a difficult coworker.

Use the "dream petition" procedure described in chapter 4 to incubate a dream by writing out in advance the guidance you hope to receive from your dreams that night. Place the petition on your nightstand, under your pillow, or on your altar. When seeking guidance from dreams, there are further steps that can have a powerful effect on the results. For dream incubation — and the insight for interpreting the dream you receive — prayer is a powerful tool.

Before your altar, address the Highest Power and pray for lucidity and vivid memory to recall the dream when you awaken.

In the name of I AM THAT I AM, I ask my Higher Self for
a dream that helps me understand my [relationship, job,

> You must have a room or a certain hour of the day where you do not know what was in the morning paper...a place where you can simply experience and bring forth what you are, and what you might be.... At first you may find nothing's happening...but if you have a sacred place and use it, take advantage of it, something will happen.
>
> ∽ Joseph Campbell

He is the innermost Self.
He is the great Lord.
He is that reveals the
purity within the heart by
means of which He,
who is pure being,
may be reached.
He is the ruler.
He is the great Light,
shining forever.

        Svetasvatara
            Upanishad

decision, situation, et cetera] so I may [solve, endure, change, et cetera] it with the principles of True Love. Give me the clarity and inspiration to interpret my dream correctly.

The next morning, follow the procedure described in chapter 4 for recording and interpreting your dream. Remember to express gratitude to your higher, sacred nature — the image of God — whenever you receive guidance through your dreams.

Going to sleep: One thinks of the holy life lived by monks and how they are taught to live each moment of their lives prayerfully. Of course, most of us do not live in an environment conducive to such concentrated dedication. However, we can mark certain touchstones during the day for little practices that remind us of our innate divine origin and selfhood. In this way, we can keep closer to the image of God within Us. Bedtime is one of those touchstones. It is an excellent opportunity to ritually end your day and ease into sleep.

A number of well-known prayers for going to sleep have comforted children for centuries. As adults, we are assured that our souls will indeed keep until morning. Bedtime is an excellent time to commemorate gratitude for the completion of the day.

Children's Bedtime Prayers

Matthew, Mark, Luke, and John,
Bless the bed that I lie upon;
Four corners to my bed,
Four angels round my head,
One to watch, and one to pray,
And two to bear my soul away.

Now I lay me down to sleep,
And pray the Lord my soul to keep.
If I should die before I wake,
I pray the Lord my soul to take.

Waking: Our mornings are filled with rituals, from throwing open the curtains to brushing our teeth. We do not consciously attribute higher meaning to these rituals, but they serve to orient us from the realm of sleep to the beginning of our day out there in the world. Instituting even a brief intentional ritual in the morning, however, helps start the day according to the principles you hold dear.

Before you dress in the morning, sit before your altar, light a candle, and intone the bell. As the sound diminishes, bow to the Source of All, vibrating in your heart as in the heart of the universe, and dedicate your day as follows:

This day I seek the door of wisdom, so I may make choices that benefit the good of all.

Now begin your day, fresh from the sacred chamber of your bedroom, your very destination when day is done.

Remembering the deceased: Sometimes a brief ritual performed after someone has passed on can help give closure to grief. Light a candle for the individual and, according to your beliefs, pray for those who have been left behind. Pray also for the departed soul, for its understanding and growth as well as for its joy in being reunited with the mind of the Creator.

Changing seasons: Celebrate the cycles of nature in your bedroom by honoring the part you play as a citizen of nature. You may, for example, celebrate the passing of summer into fall. Consider performing a celebration when setting the clock forward in spring or back in the fall.

Performing a "sick in bed" healing ritual: Use this ritual when someone in the house is sick in bed. Light a healing candle (a new candle only used for this purpose) and use a healing aromatherapy scent (you will need to consult an aromatherapy book geared for illness). You can also make soup as part of the ritual and use a healing prayer. Bring a plant into the bedroom of the patient to promote clean, oxygen-rich air and to symbolize health. You can also incorporate healing music.

Telling bedtime stories: Many people have used reading to relax before sleep. In this ritual, make it a point to read aloud

**The Ten Perfections
of Buddhism**

Giving

Duty

Renunciation

Insight

Courage

Patience

Truth

Resolution

Loving-kindness

Serenity

Come and see:
The blessed Holy One
does not place his abode
in any place where male
and female are not
found together.
Blessings are found only
in a place where male
and male are found,
a human being is only
called Adam
when male and female
are as one.

    *The Zohar

before you go to sleep. Partners may alternate on different nights or during each session. Read some uplifting or inspiring passage or poem. If you are without a partner, read aloud to yourself.

Writing a gratitude list: Gratitude is the key to our happiness on every level, because without gratitude, we take what we have for granted, especially the "unearned" blessings. These are the broad circumstances of station into which we were born or that come to us through no effort of our own.

Before going to sleep at night, recall three events or experiences of the day for which you are grateful. Think of the lessons you have learned from the trials of your day and how they have made you stronger. Write them down in a "gratitude journal" and keep the journal to read whenever you are feeling low. Keep the journal on your nightstand or in the drawer of your altar.

Striving toward a goal: Whether we desire healing for a loved one, a better job, a new house, or a loving partner, everyone has goals they want to achieve. Create a ritual in which you affirm your goal by daily lighting a candle dedicated to that goal, and let it burn for the time it takes to meditate. Gather together some photos, drawings, or create a collage that depicts the goal, and visualize the fulfillment of that goal in your meditation.

Some other accomplishments and rites of passage that can be celebrated in the sacred bedroom include

- Graduation

- Conception or birth of a child

- Marriage

- Job change

- A move into a new home

Finally, once a month, have a massage therapist come to your bedroom, set up, and give you a massage with aromatherapy, candlelight, and soothing music. Prepare for the massage with a simple ritual dedicating the massage to your better health and a release from stress. (Of course, if your bedroom is small, you can move this part of the ritual into a larger room.)

GOOD NIGHT

To people who have a long-standing spiritual practice, whether it be attending weekly church services, meditation, or some other form of personalized worship, the principles presented in *The Sacred Bedroom* become second nature. Most of us know that we should treat others as we would have them treat us: This is the Golden Rule. If you adhere to the tenets of a traditional organized religion, there is no reason why you cannot keep those tenets in your bedroom by taking whatever steps you wish. If altars are not part of your faith, eliminate the altar. Use whatever symbols express, for you, your religious faith. If interpreting dreams is not sanctioned, you can still pray before you go to sleep that the Lord protect and guide your dreams. Anyone at all can benefit from creating a sacred bedroom.

If you are new to a formal spiritual path — aligning yourself with a set of spiritual ideals and consciously practicing them — the following guidance can be helpful in applying the five basic bedroom principles listed in the previous section. These guidelines can help you create a nurturing practice and engender positive new habits.

Every night, try to get a good night's sleep. Make it a priority because a good night's sleep is beneficial to your general good health, energy level, and mental acuity. A good sleep will therefore help you cope with whatever is in store for you the following day. It will help you in your work, whatever it may be, but also in your social experiences. A sharp, rested mind can better accommodate people's feelings and judge situations more clearly. Whether you are an employee or an employer, you can be more productive and cheerful, compassionate, and supportive to others. A good sleep can enhance all your relationships. Being well rested also helps you look and feel more attractive.

By all means, discover and enjoy your senses in the sacred bedroom, but do not become lost in them. Go into the still place inside periodically through meditation. Step away from strong feelings and sensory stimulations. Remember that while our sensual side is part of our overall makeup, it is all too easy to slip

Bedtime Story

In the first half of the twentieth century, eight out of ten married couples slept in double beds. Popular in France and somewhat so in England, they were not shown on American TV during the 1950s and 1960s.

into the illusion that you can live by pleasure alone. Balance is the key.

The sacred bedroom can also help you manage present, future, and even past romances, if you are willing to be sensible and spiritual about them. Before we discussed the role of sex in the sacred bedroom, we looked at the mythical and illusory aspects of being in love as well as the potential spiritual connection among the symbols of romance. Keep in mind the virtues upheld by Sir Lancelot and Guinevere. Consider a deeper spiritual intent for the symbols of romance, hearts and flowers, dinner for two.

Your sacred bedroom attitude can be especially helpful if you are dating. If you are looking for a serious, long-lasting relationship, be sure to approach your goal from heart-centered love, while keeping your mind attuned to True Love. In this way, your desire for a partner, with or without sexual contact, will free you to make a positive choice. It will help you stay in touch with your authentic self — and thereby attract the best partner for you. If you are stressed, depressed, or desperate, you will attract one type of person. When you are centered, rested, being genuine with yourself and others, you will attract quite another.

With True Love as the engine of your being, you are able to enjoy romance in a more balanced way. Take your time to get to know him or her. Find the authentic self of the one you love, and treat that person with compassion, even if all your senses are on fire with adoration. This is approaching your love affair from a place of wisdom. You will be able to avoid many of the emotional ups and downs, the deceptions, and discoveries that often accompany love affairs.

If you are sexually active with your partner, try to honor sex as a sacred experience. This will free you to greater, longer-lasting pleasure, while releasing you in True Love that is easier to apply to people and situations after you have experienced it during sex — the most pleasurable act. Elevating your concept of sex above the physical is elevating your concept of *life* above the physical. This is your growing awareness of the soul — consciousness of the energy beneath it all — and awareness of light behind all your understanding. Conquering sex by cleaning it up, refining it in

> To truly find God, truth needs to be found independently from the opinions of others. The truth has to be found in our hearts.
>
> ꙮ A. H. Almaas

spiritual understanding, can help you transcend the push and pull of your emotions, and help you know your rightful place in the universe.

After a period of experimenting in your sacred bedroom, return to the self-evaluation questions in chapter 1. If you recorded your answers in a journal, read them over and see if your answers have changed. All the reminders of a sacred environment now surround you when you go to sleep at night and wake in the morning. Those reminders alone can prompt the heart to open and the mind to track on the Divine. They can inspire a prayer, a pang of motivation for expressing kindness throughout the day, and perhaps a flutter of gratitude in the heart. The more you use your bedroom space for spiritual practice, the more benefits begin to mount. You become an active participant in the spiritual universe, a partner with the Creator, whose image resides within you. You can reveal it all, within yourself, in your sacred bedroom.

> The self resides within
> the lotus of the heart.
> Knowing this,
> devoted to the self,
> the sage enters daily
> that holy sanctuary.
>
> ∽ Chandogya Upanishad

It All Happened in Bed

- During World War II, Winston Churchill issued orders from his bed.
- John Lennon and Yoko Ono once stayed in bed a year in order to "Give Peace a Chance."
- After lying down one day, Einstein saw $E = mc^2$ flash on the inside of his eyelids.
- Once, while in a slump, golfer Jack Nicklaus dreamed of a new way to grip his club. He tried it, and it improved his game.

Resource
Directory

AIR PURIFICATION

AIRWISE
Waterwise, Inc.
P.O. Box 494000
Leesburg, FL 34749
(800) 874-9028
www.waterwise.com

PURE & NATURAL SYSTEMS, INC.
5836 Lincoln Avenue
Morton Grove, IL 60053
(800) 237-9199
www.purenatural.com

ESSENTIAL OILS

EARTH ESSENTIALS
P.O. Box 35284
Sarasota, Florida 34242
(800) 370-3220

NELSON BACH USA, LTD.
100 Research Drive
Wilmington, MA 01887
(800) 319-9151
www.nelsonbach.com
Supplier of Bach flower essences

THE ESSENTIAL OIL COMPANY
1719 SE Umatilla Street
Portland, OR 97202
(800) 729-5912
www.essentialoil.com

NATIONAL ASSOCIATION FOR
HOLISTIC AROMATHERAPY
P.O. Box 17622
Boulder, CO 80307
(800) 566-6735
www.naha.org
Information on registered therapists

FENG SHUI/HOLISTIC DECORATING

EARTH DESIGN
P.O. Box 530725
Miami Shores, FL 33153
(305) 756-6426
www.jamilin.com

FENG SHUI DESIGNS
P.O. Box 399
Nevada City, CA 95959
(800) 551-2482
www.fengshuidesigns.com

FENG SHUI INSTITUTE OF AMERICA
P.O. Box 488
Wabasso, FL 32970
(407) 588-9900
www.windwater.com

FENG SHUI WAREHOUSE, INC.
P.O. Box 6689
San Diego, CA 92166
(800) 399-1599
www.fengshuiwarehouse.com

NANCY SANTOPIETRO & ASSOCIATES
1684 80th Street
Brooklyn, NY 11214
(718) 256-2640; or
2366 Eastlake Avenue E.
Seattle, WA 98102
(206) 320-9660
Feng shui consultations and
workshops

FULL-SPECTRUM LIGHTING

NATURAL FULL-SPECTRUM LIGHTING
1939 Richvale Street
Houston, TX 77062
(888)900-6830
www.naturallighting.com

FULL SPECTRUM SOLUTIONS
4880 Brooklyn Road
Jackson, MI 49201
(888) 574-7014
www.fullspectrumsolutions.com

GENERAL PRODUCTS
Eco Essentials
600 Windfields Street
Denton, TX 76201
(940) 484-9101
www.ecoessentials.com

REAL GOODS
Customer Service
360 Interlocken Blvd., Suite 300
Broomfield, CO 80021-3440
(800) 762-7325
www.realgoods.com
Products for an ecologically
sustainable future (see website for
retail locations)

LAUNDRY AND CLEANING PRODUCTS

EARTH FRIENDLY PRODUCTS
44 Greenbay Road
Winnetka, IL 60093
(800) 335-ECOS (3267)
www.ecos.com

MOUNTAIN GREEN
7399 S. Tucson Way
Englewood, CO 80112
(888) 878-5781
www.mtngreen.com

PLANET SOLUTIONS
5601 N. Powerline Road
Ft. Lauderdale, FL 33309
(888) 313-6183
www.planetsolutions.org

MEDITATION INSTRUCTION

THE ASSOCIATION FOR RESEARCH AND
ENLIGHTENMENT, INC.
215 67th Street
Virginia Beach, VA 23451-2061
(800) 333-4499
www.edgarcayce.org

CAMBRIDGE INSIGHT MEDITATION
CENTER
331 Broadway
Cambridge, MA 02139
(617) 441-9038

CAMBRIDGE ZEN CENTER
199 Auburn Street
Cambridge, MA 02139
(617) 576-3229
www.cambridgezen.com

BODY/MIND RESTORATION RETREAT,
ITHACA ZEN CENTER
56 Lieb Road
Spencer, NY 14883
(607) 272-0694 (phone/fax)
www.retreatsonline.com/usa/newy
ork/ithacazen.htm

ELAT CHAYYIM: A CENTER FOR
HEALING AND RENEWAL
99 Mill Hood Road
Accord, NY 12404
(800) 398-2630
www.elatchayyim.org

ESALEN INSTITUTE
Highway 1
Big Sur, CA 93920-9616
(408) 667-3000
www.esalen.org

NAROPA UNIVERSITY
2130 Arapahoe Avenue
Boulder, CO 80302
(800) 772-6951
www.naropa.edu

NEW LIFE HEALTH CENTER, INC.
12 Harris Avenue
Jamaica Plain, MA 02130
(617) 524-9551
www.anewlife.com

NEW YORK OPEN CENTER, INC.
83 Spring Street
New York, NY 10012
(212) 219-2527
www.opencenter.org

OMEGA INSTITUTE FOR HOLISTIC
STUDIES
260 Lake Drive
Rhinebeck, NY 12572
 (914) 266-4444
www.omega-inst.org

SAN FRANCISCO ZEN CENTER
300 Page Street
San Francisco, CA 94102
(415) 863-3136
www.sfzc.com

SOUTHERN DHARMA RETREAT CENTER
1661 West Road
Hot Springs, NC 28743
(828) 622-7112
www.main.nc.us/sdrc.htm

SPIRIT ROCK MEDITATION CENTER
P.O. Box 169
Woodacre, CA 94973
(415) 488-0164
www.spiritrock.org

MEDITATION SUPPLIES

CAROLINA MORNING DESIGNS
P.O. Box 509
Micaville, NC 28755
(828) 675-0490
www.zafu.net
Meditation cushions and benches

CHÖPA IMPORTS
P.O. Box 21516
Boulder, CO 80308
(303) 499-0757
www.chopa.com
Asian arts, Buddhist, meditation,
and altar supplies

DHARMACRAFTS
405 Waltham Street, Suite 234
Lexington, MA 02421
(800) 794-9862
www.dharmacrafts.com
Meditation cushions and benches,
bells and gongs, incense and burners, prayer beads, statues

SAMADHI CUSHIONS
30 Church Street
Barnet, VT 05821
(802) 633-4440
www.samadicushions.com
Mats, cushions, gomden, zafu

SHASTA ABBEY
3724 Summit Drive
Mount Shasta, CA 96067
(800) 653-3315
www.obcon.org
Gongs, temple instruments,
incense, cushions, benches

NATURAL PAINTS

NATURAL HOME PRODUCTS.COM
P.O. Box 1677
Sebastopol, CA 95473
(707) 824-0914
www.monitor.net/~nathome

SINAN COMPANY
P.O. Box 857
Davis, CA 95616-0857
(530) 753-3104
www.dcn.davis.ca.us/go/sinan
Natural building materials

THE OLD FASHIONED MILK PAINT CO.
436 Main Street
Groton, MA 01450
(978) 448-6336
www.milkpaint.com

ORGANIC BEDDING

ATLANTIC EARTHWORKS
21 Winters Lane
Catonsville, MD 21228
(800) 323-2811
www.atlanticearthworks.com

NIRVANA SAFE HAVEN
3441 Golden Rain Road
Walnut Creek, CA 94595
(800) 968-9355
www.nontoxic.com

TERRA VERDE
120 Wooster Street
New York, NY 10012
(212) 925-4533
www.terraverde.com

PRAYER/MEDITATION

CHRISTIAN MEDITATION CENTER
1080 West Irving Park Road
Roselle, IL 60172
(630) 351-2613

CONTEMPLATIVE OUTREACH
10 Park Place, Suite 2B
P.O. Box 737
Butler, NJ 07405
(973) 838-3384
www.centeringprayer.com

FELLOWSHIP IN PRAYER
291 Witherspoon Street
Princeton, NJ 08542-9946
(609) 924-6863

HEART OF STILLNESS RETREATS
P.O. Box 106
Jamestown, CO 80455
(303) 459-3431

SLEEP/DREAMS

ASSOCIATION FOR THE STUDY OF
DREAMS
P.O. Box 1592
Merced, CA 95341
(209) 724-0889
www.asdreams.org

BETTER SLEEP GUIDE
P.O. Box 19534
Alexandria, VA 22320-0534
(sixteen-page brochure about
sleep-health connection, mattress
guidelines, et cetera)

DELANEY & FLOWERS DREAM CENTER
337 Spruce Street
San Francisco, CA 94118
(415) 587-3424
(classes and programs for dream
analysis)

SLEEP MEDICINE ASSOCIATES OF TEXAS
8140 Walnut Hill Lane
Dallas, TX 75231
(214) 750-7776
www.sleepmed.com

TANTRISM/SEXUALITY

SKYDANCING INSTITUTE
20 Sunnyside Avenue, Suite A219
Mill Valley, CA 94941
(415) 457-4877

HEALING TAO INSTITUTE
P.O. Box 9312
Austin, TX 78765
(800) 432-5826
www.healingtaoinstitute.com

YOGA/MEDITATION

INTEGRAL YOGA®
Satchidananda Ashram – Yogaville
Rt. 1, Box 1720
Buckingham, VA 23921
(800) 858-9642
www.yogaville.org

SELF-REALIZATION FELLOWSHIP
3880 San Rafael Avenue
Los Angeles, CA 90065
(323) 225-2471
www.yogananda-srf.org

Permissions Acknowledgments

Grateful acknowledgment is given to the following publishers and copyright holders for permission to reprint the quotations in *The Sacred Bedroom:*

From *9¹/₂ Mystics: The Kabbala Today* by Rabbi Herbert Weiner. Copyright © 1969, 1992 by Herbert Weiner. Reprinted by permission of Henry Holt & Co., LLC.

From *Altars: Bring Sacred Shrines into Your Everyday Life* by Denise Linn. Copyright © 1999 by Denise Linn. Reprinted by permission of Ballantine Books, a division of Random House, Inc.

From *Feng Shui: The Chinese Art of Placement* by Sarah Rossbach. Copyright © 1983 by Sarah Rossbach. Reprinted by permission of Dutton, a division of Penguin Putnam Inc.

From *The Feng Shui of Love: Arrange Your Home to Attract and Hold Love* by T. Raphael Simons. Copyright © 2000 by T. Raphael Simons. Reprinted by permission of The Crown Publishing Group.

From *A History of God: The 4,000-Year Quest of Judaism, Christianity and Islam* by Karen Armstrong. Copyright © 1993 by Karen Armstrong. Reprinted by permission of Ballantine Books, a division of Random House, Inc.

From *A Home for the Soul: A Guide for Dwelling with Spirit and Imagination* by Anthony Lawlor. Copyright © 1997 by Anthony Lawlor. Reprinted by permission of Clarkson Potter, a division of The Crown Publishing Group.

From *House as a Mirror of Self: Exploring the Deeper Meaning of Home* by Clare Cooper Marcus. Copyright © 1997 by Clare Cooper Marcus. Reprinted by permission of Conari Press.

Bibliography

Alexander, Jane. *Rituals for Sacred Living.* New York: Sterling Publishing Co., Inc., 1999.

Anand, Margot. *The Art of Everyday Ecstasy: The Seven Tantric Keys for Bringing Passion, Spirit, and Joy into Every Part of Your Life.* New York: Broadway Books, 1998.

————. *The Art of Sexual Ecstasy: The Path of Sacred Sexuality for Western Lovers.* Los Angeles: Jeremy P. Tarcher, Inc., 1989.

Ardinger, Barbara, Ph.D. *Practicing the Presence of the Goddess.* Novato, Calif.: New World Library, 2000.

Armstrong, Karen. *A History of God: The 4,000-Year Quest of Judaism, Christianity and Islam.* New York: Ballantine Books, 1993.

Barks, Coleman and Michael Green. *The Illuminated Prayer: The Five-Times Prayer of the Sufis.* New York: The Ballantine Publishing Group, 2000.

Bates, Robert. *Sacred Sex: Erotic Writings from the Religions of the World.* New York: HarperCollins Publishers, Inc., 1993.

Bennett, Julienne and Mimi Lubbermann, eds. *Where the Heart Is: A Celebration of Home.* Novato, Calif.: New World Library, and Berkeley, Calif.: Wildcat Canyon Press, 1995.

Besserman, Perle. *The Shambhala Guide to Kabbalah and Jewish Mysticism.* Boston: Shambhala Publications, Inc., 1997.

Bharati, Agehananda. *The Tantric Tradition.* Garden City, N.Y.: Anchor Books, 1970.

Borys, Henry James. *The Sacred Fire: Love as a Spiritual Path.* San Francisco: HarperSanFrancisco, 1994.

Bouquet, A. C. *Sacred Books of the World.* Baltimore: Penguin Books, 1967.

Burton, Richard F., trans. *The Kama Sutra of Vatsyayana.* New York: E. P. Dutton & Co., 1964.

Camphausen, Rufus C. *The Encyclopedia of Erotic Wisdom.* Rochester, Vt.: Inner Traditions International, 1991.

Chöpel, Gedün. *Tibetan Arts of Love: Sex, Orgasm, and Spiritual Healing.* Trans. Jeffrey Hopkins. Ithaca, N.Y.: Snow Lion Publications, 1992.

Chopra, Deepak, M.D. *How to Know God: The Soul's Journey into the Mystery of Mysteries.* New York: Harmony Books, 2000.

————. *Restful Sleep: The Complete Mind/Body Program for Overcoming Insomnia.* New York: Harmony Books, 1994.

Crim, Keith, gen. ed. *Abingdon Dictionary of Living Religions.* Nashville, Tenn.: Abingdon Press, 1981.

Collins, Terah Kathrun. *The Western Guide to Feng Shui: Room by Room.* Carlsbad, Calif.: Hay House, 1999.

Cunningham, Scott. *Sacred Sleep: Dreams and the Divine.* Santa Cruz, Calif.: Crossing Press, 1990.

De Becker, Raymond. *The Understanding of Dreams and Their Influence on the History of Man.* New York: Bell Publishing Company, 1965.

Delaney, Gayle, Ph.D. *In Your Dreams: Falling, Flying and Other Dream Themes.* San Francisco: HarperSanFrancisco, 1997.

Donnelly, Dody H. *Radical Love: An Approach to Sexual Spirituality.* Minneapolis, Minn.: Winston Press, Inc., 1984.

Doyle, Brendan. *Meditations with Julian of Norwich.* Santa Fe, N.M.: Bear and Company, Inc., 1983.

Easwaran, Eknath. *Meditation: An Eight-Point Program for Translating Spiritual Ideals into Everyday Life.* Tomales, Calif.: Nilgiri Press, 1991.

Edstrom, KRS. *Conquering Stress: The Skills You Need to Succeed in the Business World.* Hauppauge, N.Y.: Barron's Educational Series, Inc., 1993.

Eisler, Riane. *The Chalice and the Blade: Our History, Our Future.* San Francisco: HarperSanFrancisco, 1987.

————. *Sacred Pleasure: Sex, Myth, and the Politics of the Body: New Paths to Power and Love.* San Francisco: HarperSanFrancisco, 1995.

Feuerstein, Georg. *Sacred Sexuality: Living the Vision of the Erotic Spirit.* New York: The Putnam Publishing Group, 1992.

Fox, Matthew. *The Coming of the Cosmic Christ.* San Francisco: Harper & Row, Publishers, Inc., 1988.

————. *One River, Many Wells: Wisdom Springing from Global Faiths.* New York: Jeremy P. Tarcher, Inc./Putnam, 2000.

Gaskell, G. A. *Dictionary of All Myths and Scriptures.* New York: Gramercy Books, 1981.

Griffiths, Bede. *Universal Wisdom: A Journey through the Sacred Wisdom of the World.* San Francisco: HarperSanFrancisco, 1994.

Hamrick, Narecia, Ph.D., and P. E. Bingeman. *Limitless Intimacy: A Guide to Spiritual Sex.* Dallas, Tex.: Elysian Press, 1990.

Hayward, Jeremy and Karen Hayward. *Sacred World: The Shambhala Way to Gentleness, Bravery, and Power.* Boston: Shambhala Publications, Inc., 1998.

Helminski, Kabir. *The Knowing Heart: A Sufi Path of Transformation.* Boston: Shambhala Publications, Inc., 1999.

Hendricks, Gay, Ph.D., and Kathlyn Hendricks, Ph.D. *Centering and the Art of Intimacy Handbook: A New Psychology of Close Relationships.* New York: Simon & Schuster, 1993.

Holzer, Hans. *The Psychic Side of Dreams.* Garden City, N.Y.: Doubleday and Company, 1976.

Isaacson, Sara. *Principles of Jewish Spirituality.* London: Thorsons, 1999.

Julian, Elizabeth Spearing, trans. *Revelations of Divine Love.* New York: Penguin USA, 1999.

Keen, Sam. *To Love and Be Loved.* New York: Bantam Books, 1997.

Kingma, Daphne Rose. *The Future of Love: The Power of the Soul in Intimate Relationships*. New York: Doubleday, 1998.

Krippner, Stanley, Ph.D., ed. *Dreamtime and Dreamwork: Decoding the Language of the Night*. Los Angeles: Jeremy P. Tarcher, Inc., 1990.

Langdon, William Chauncy. *Everyday Things in American Life 1776–1876*. New York: Charles Scribner's Sons, 1941.

Lawlor, Anthony. *A Home for the Soul*. New York: Clarkson Potter, 1997.

———. *The Temple in the House: Finding the Sacred in Everyday Architecture*. New York: Jeremy P. Tarcher, Inc./Putnam, 1994.

Lee, Victoria, Ph.D. *Soulful Sex: Opening Your Heart, Body, and Spirit to Lifelong Passion*. Berkeley, Calif.: Conari Press, 1996.

Linn, Denise. *Altars: Bringing Sacred Shrines into Your Everyday Life*. New York: Ballantine Books, 1999.

———. *Sacred Space: Clearing and Enhancing the Energy of Your Home*. New York: Ballantine Books, 1995.

MacKenzie, Norman. *Dreams and Dreaming*. New York: The Vanguard Press, Inc., 1965.

Mann, A. T. and Jane Lyle. *Sacred Sexuality*. Rockport, Mass.: Element Books, 1994.

Marcus, Clare Cooper. *House as a Mirror of Self: Exploring the Deeper Meaning of Home*. Berkeley, Calif.: Conari Press, 1997.

Michaels, Stase. *The Bedside Guide to Dreams*. New York: Ballantine Books, 1995.

Moore, Thomas. *Original Self: Living with Paradox and Authenticity*. New York: HarperCollins Publishers, Inc., 2000.

———. *Soul Mates: Honoring the Mysteries of Love and Relationship*. New York, HarperCollins Publishers, Inc., 1994.

Moran, Victoria. *Shelter for the Spirit: How to Create Your Own Haven in a Hectic World*. New York: HarperCollins, 1998.

Munro, Eleanor, ed. *Wedding Readings: Centuries of Writing and Rituals on Love and Marriage*. New York: Viking/Penguin Books USA, Inc., 1989.

Nik, Douglas and Penny Slinger. *Sexual Secrets: The Alchemy of Ecstasy*. New York: Destiny Books, 1979.

Olson, Stuart Alve, trans. *Cultivating the Ch'i*. St. Paul, Minn.: Dragon Door Publications, 1992.

Panati, Charles. *Sacred Origins of Profound Things*. New York: Penguin/Arkana, 1996.

Peterson, Roland. *Everyone Is Right: A New Look at Comparative Religion and Its Relation to Science*. Marina del Rey, Calif.: DeVorss & Company, 1986.

Post, Steven. *The Modern Book of Feng Shui: Vitality and Harmony for the Home and Office*. New York: Dell Publishing, 1998.

Powers, John. *Introduction to Tibetan Buddhism*. Ithaca, N.Y.: Snow Lion Publications, 1995.

Premananda, Swami. *The Sanctity of the Senses*. Washington, D.C.: Self-Realization Fellowship, 1948.

Rossbach, Sarah. *Feng Shui: The Chinese Art of Placement*. New York: Penguin/Arkana, 1991.

SantoPietro, Nancy. *Feng Shui: Harmony by Design*. New York: The Berkley Publishing Group, 1996.

Schiller, David and Carol Schiller. *Aromatherapy for Mind and Body*. New York: Sterling Publishing Co., Inc., 1996.

Simons, T. Raphael. *The Feng Shui of Love*. New York: Three Rivers Press, 2000.

Smith, Huston. *Forgotten Truth: The Common Vision of the World's Religions*. San Francisco: Harper-SanFrancisco, 1992.

———. *The World's Religions*. San Francisco: HarperSanFrancisco, 1992.

Sovatsky, Stewart. *Passions of Innocence: Tantric Celibacy and the Mysteries of Eros*. Rochester, Vt.: Destiny Books, 1994.

Stevens, John. *Lust for Enlightenment: Buddhism and Sex*. Boston: Shambhala Publications, Inc., 1994.

Tannahill, Reay. *Sex in History*. New York: Stein and Day Publishers, 1980.

Trevelyan, Joanna. *Holistic Home: Creating an Environment for Physical and Spiritual Well-Being*. New York: Sterling Publishing Co., Inc., 1998.

Trungpa, Chögyam. *The Myth of Freedom and the Way of Meditation*. Berkeley: Shambhala Publications, Inc., 1976.

Van de Castle, Robert L., Ph.D. *Our Dreaming Mind*. New York: Ballantine Books, 1994.

Wehr, Gerhard. *The Mystical Marriage: Symbol and Meaning of the Human Experience*. Wellingborough, England: The Aquarian Press, 1990.

Weiner, Herbert. *9 1/2 Mystics: The Kabbala Today*. New York: Macmillan Publishing Co., 1992.

White, Judith and Karen Downes. *Aromatherapy for Scentual Awareness*. New York: Crown, 1992.

Wile, Douglas. *The Art of the Bedchamber: The Chinese Sexual Yoga Classics, Including Women's Solo Meditation Texts*. Albany, N.Y.: State University of New York Press, 1992.

Wolkstein, Diane. *The First Love Stories: From Isis and Osiris to Tristan and Iseult*. New York: HarperCollins Publishers, Inc., 1991.

Worwood, Susan. *Essential Aromatherapy: A Pocket Guide to Essential Oils and Aromatherapy*. Novato, Calif.: New World Library, 1995.

Worwood, Valerie Ann. *The Complete Book of Essential Oils & Aromatherapy*. Novato, Calif.: New World Library, 1991.

———. *The Fragrant Mind: Aromatherapy for Personality, Mind, Mood, and Emotion*. Novato, Calif.: New World Library, 1996.

Yogananda, Paramahansa. *Wine of the Mystic — The Rubaiyat of Omar Khayyam: A Spiritual Interpretation*. Trans. Edward Fitzgerald. Los Angeles: Self-Realization Fellowship, 1994.

Zaleski, Philip and Paul Kaufman. *Gifts of the Spirit: Living the Wisdom of the Great Religious Traditions*. New York: HarperCollins Publishers, Inc., 1998.

Index

About the Author

Jon Robertson is an editor, journalist, and speaker who has spent a lifetime studying religion, philosophy, and Eastern thought. He is co-author of *The Sacred Kitchen,* with his wife Robin, and author of *The Golden Thread of Oneness: A Journey Inward to the Universal Consciousness.* A produced playwright and lyricist, he lives and works in Virginia Beach, Virginia.

New World Library is dedicated to
publishing books and cassettes that inspire
and challenge us to improve the quality
of our lives and our world.

Our books and cassettes are available
at bookstores everywhere.
For a complete catalog, contact:

NEW WORLD LIBRARY
14 Pamaron Way
Novato, California 94949

Phone: (415) 884-2100
Fax: (415) 884-2199

Or call toll free: (800) 972-6657
Catalog requests: Ext. 50
Ordering: Ext. 52

E-mail: escort@nwlib.com
Website: newworldlibrary.com